EMERSON
AND
UNIVERSAL
MIND

EMERSON

AND

UNIVERSAL MIND

Richard G. Geldard

Larson Publications
Burdett, New York

ISBN-10: 1-936012-64-2
ISBN-13: 978-193601264-0
eISBN-10: 1-936012-65-0
eISBN-13: 978-1-936012-65-0

Library of Congress Control Number: 2013941417

Publisher's Cataloging-In-Publication Data
(Prepared by The Donohue Group, Inc.)

Geldard, Richard G., 1935-
    Emerson and universal mind / Richard G. Geldard.

    p. ; cm.

    Issued also as an ebook.
    ISBN-13: 978-1-936012-64-0
    ISBN-10: 1-936012-64-2

    1. Neoplatonism. 2. Emerson, Ralph Waldo, 1803-1882--Philosophy.
3. Transcendentalism (New England) I. Title.

B517 .G45 2013
141.2   2013941417

Published by Larson Publications
4936 State Route 414
Burdett, New York 14818 USA

http://larsonpublications.com

23 22 21 20 19 8 17 16 15 14 13

10 9 8 7 6 5 4 3 2 1

Contents

PART I

The Chief Task of Emerson's Life

Emerson Returns to Harvard

In 1867, thirty years after Emerson delivered his Phi Beta Kappa address at Harvard entitled "The American Scholar," he was asked to deliver a second address to the same honors society. Normally, we would not think this a date worth reporting, except that during those thirty years Emerson had not been invited to speak on any occasion at his alma mater, because his address to the graduates of Divinity College in 1838 had so angered the faculty of the college that he was declared *persona non grata*.

The irony of course is that in those thirty years, Emerson became an important and much admired figure in American letters. Some called him the Seer of Concord. After 1850 he was also a leader in the movement to abolish slavery. Such was his national reputation as a writer, lecturer, and public figure that Harvard grew increasingly embarrassed to have treated him in such a shabby manner.

His crime in 1838 was his criticism of the Unitarian interpretation of Christian theology, which also was ironic as the Unitarians at the time were considered the most liberal and least judgmental branch of Christian belief. Emerson's sermon to the half dozen graduates, faculty, and guests on that July evening was less about theological arguments than a plea to the students to speak from experience and not from tradition to their congregations. This practical and useful advice was fine, but then Emerson went on to say that Jesus "belonged to the true race of prophets. He saw with open eye the mystery of the soul. Drawn by its severe harmony, ravished with its beauty, he lived in it, and had his being there." The faculty squirmed. Emerson then took the bold step of putting words into the mouth of Jesus:

He said, in this jubilee of sublime emotion, "I am divine. Through me, God acts; through me, speaks. Would you see God, see me; or, see thee, when thou also thinkest as I now think." But what a distortion did his doctrine and memory suffer in the same, in the next, and the following ages! There is no doctrine of the Reason which will bear to be taught by the Understanding. The understanding caught this high chant from the poet's lips, and said, in the next age, "This was Jehovah come down out of heaven. I will kill you, if you say he was a man."

The faculty of Divinity College declared Emerson a heretic and as a result he was effectively banned from any further formal association with Harvard. Now, however, in 1867, Harvard found itself out of step with the rest of the country, or at least with the literate members of society who treasured Emerson's works and gathered to hear his lectures during those thirty years. Emerson not only gave the Phi Beta Kappa address that year but also was made a Harvard Overseer and received an honorary degree of Doctor of Letters. He had officially been forgiven his earlier heresy, although no doubt there was still grumbling over at Divinity College.

Then, in 1870, the young new president of Harvard College, Charles Eliot, in an effort to expand and strengthen the study of philosophy, established what he called the University Lectures and invited Emerson, among others, to give a series of eighteen lectures of his own choosing. For Emerson, this was an opportunity to summarize his life-long vision of Idealism, a vision which had formed the central set of principles in what came to be known as New England Transcendentalism.

Emerson's experience as part of this course was hardly comfortable. He was under tremendous pressure to work quickly and to fit his material into the overall series of lectures. As it turned out, his proposed series of eighteen became seven and the material itself was not a survey of world philosophy but a summation of Emerson's theories on the nature of the mind. It is also ironic that over those thirty years since the Divinity School Address, which had been requested by the students, the new generation of Divinity scholars petitioned the college to be able to attend the Emerson lectures without paying the fee. But they were turned down, or else the lecture room would have been more populated.

Over the years scholars have tended to minimize, even to the extent of total neglect, what remains of these late lectures, assuming that Emerson's intellectual and expressive powers had diminished, rendering this material irrelevant. However, his good friend, editor, and biographer James Elliot Cabot, whose task it was to gather Emerson's papers into some order, said this of Harvard's invitation to lecture: "Emerson welcomed the proposal as an opportunity for taking up and completing his sketches of the 'Natural History of the Intellect,' which he appears to have regarded as the chief task of his life."[1]

Given Cabot's observation here, this commentary intends to give serious attention to what remains of these lectures in order to fill a valuable gap in Emerson's attention to the laws of the mind. By extension it also provides a more accurate and complete assessment of Transcendentalism as an important contribution to the history and influence of American philosophy.

As Ronald Bosco and Joel Myerson attest in their two-volume *Later Lectures,* Emerson worked on this "chief task of his life" through most of his writing and lecture career. Even though we have only fragments from the aborted lecture series Emerson gave to the philosophy students at Harvard in 1871, we do have substantial material to fill out his central thesis, a hint of which he gave when he said (quoted in the excerpt above), "There is no doctrine of the Reason which will bear to be taught by the Understanding."

Standing alone, this sentence is perplexing, partly because of Emerson's distinctive denotation of both Reason and Understanding, both words capitalized to signify their abstract and philosophical underpinning. But more on this below. In order to complete this introduction, we have to complete the background.

Early references to mind, what would later be "The Natural History of Intellect,"[2] occur in the major works, namely *Nature* and *Essays I* and *II.* The famous opening sentence from "History," "There is one mind common to all individual men," was his first shot across the bow of the warship Materialism. Emerson's intent there was to assert that the human story is the history of that one mind and is not the mundane account of dates and events that we encounter.

But these statements of principle were not systematic nor could they be called philosophy in the traditional sense of that discipline. It was not really until 1848, when Emerson took his second trip to England and Europe, that he made an effort to formalize his views of the structure and functions of mind. He prepared lectures for delivery in England and felt rightly that

the British would demand a more formal and structured articulation of his views. This effort produced a series which began
with "The Powers and Laws of Thought."

Emerson's agile wit takes center stage in the opening paragraph of "Powers and Laws" when he observes that he enjoyed
listening to scientific lectures in London and Paris and could
not help admiring "the irresponsible security and happiness of
the attitude of the naturalist, sure of admiration for his facts,"
and he decided that he too could make similar claims about the
laws of the mind as also being facts of Natural History.

What may appear to be a gentle jab at certainty typical of
materialistic scientific assumptions, Emerson wanted also to
suggest that such certainty is not justified and that truth is not
arrived at so easily. Indeed, within two years Darwin would
publish and call into question many of these assumptions. For
physics, revision would take a little longer, but the result would
be would be more revolutionary, even to the point of threatening
the very ground of the materialist world view. In the meantime,
Emerson would keep to his task, writing and giving lectures to
mixed reviews, ever feeling unsatisfied with his efforts but always
sure of his essential facts.

Other lectures during this period are "Mind and Manners
in the Nineteenth Century," numbers I, II, and III. Then, later,
beginning 1858, "Natural Methods of Mental Philosophy," lectures I through VI. These lectures were frequently revised and
retitled, depending on his audience. His effort was always to
make them accessible, which for a man of such natural eloquence was not always easy or successful.

Susan Sontag once famously said that she never read com-
mentaries, but only original writings. Valid, of course, but with
Emerson, the archive is so huge, so dispersed in texts some of
which are scarcely available, that commentary seems not only

valid but necessary, especially if it results in drawing the reader to the original material, to Emerson himself in his own words. It is to that end that this commentary is offered on Emerson and the nature of mind.

The effort we are undertaking in examining Emerson's later work is, frankly, difficult work. He warns us that approaching this subject is like trying to swim *up* Niagara Falls. The effort is so challenging (or impossible where Niagara is involved) because we have to penetrate Emerson's eloquence, his extraordinary gift for language. He is one of our foremost thinkers and expressive writers, weaving as he does such complex designs as to suggest some magical Persian carpet which we expect to be able to sit on and fly to great heights.

But perhaps that impression is false and, as he says himself, all this so-called complexity is a "play in natural action." And what is that? Certainly it is to be content to plot a fragmentary curve in order to find the immense arc of the higher mind of his genius and appreciate its universal nature and character. In this case the plotting of the curve involves taking note of isolated facts in our own experience in order to discover that these dots do in fact plot a curve far beyond ordinary experience to give us a glimpse of the powers of the mind.

Therefore, to appreciate and perhaps even grasp his meaning, it may not be necessary to attempt the swim up the Falls but instead to stand in its mist and estimate its power and know that it is real. Emerson gives us two pieces of inspiration to help us undertake this journey. The first is from Zoroaster: "Let the depth, the immortal depth of your soul, lead you." And a saying from Pythagoras: "Remember to be sober, and to be disposed to believe; for these are the nerves of wisdom."

2:

The Principles

The principle of Idealism developed by Emerson starting with *Nature* in 1836 made a subtle distinction between religion and philosophy. As the years went on, his writing made that distinction a bright line rather than a subtle difference. Twenty years later, in his 1858 essay "Powers of the Mind," he made an unacknowledged reference to Emmanuel Swedenborg when he wrote "To construct a philosophy is nothing more than to give the best attention to the operation of one's own mind."

We are reminded, for example, of his famous sentence from "Self-Reliance," "Nothing is, at last, sacred but the integrity of your own mind." In this formulation Emerson put the emphasis on the integrity of the mind, meaning that our sense of the sacred emerges first from a mind that is whole, integrated and not fragmented. As such, it is an example of the virtues and benefits of spiritual work.

In the Swedenborg formulation, the emphasis shifts to the intention to "construct a philosophy," something Emerson was early on hesitant to propose. He wanted to avoid creating a system as much as he wanted to avoid creating an Emersonian religion. But the idea of constructing a philosophy of mind was exactly what Idealism was all about, and Emerson needed to

put that principle out in front of his subsequent writings on the
subject—which, as we shall see, were extensive.

1. THE FIRST PRINCIPLE.

Emerson set out to offer a viable alternative to Materialism.
As he pointed out, distinctions between religion and philosophy are not the only areas of human endeavor for debate. The
larger distinction in philosophy is the fundamental difference
between Idealism and Materialism. Emerson wrote in "The
Transcendentalist,"

> *As thinkers, mankind have ever divided into two sects,*
> *Materialists and Idealists; the first class founding on experi-*
> *ence, the second on consciousness; the first class beginning to*
> *think from the data of the senses, the second class perceive that*
> *the senses are not final, and say, the senses give us representa-*
> *tions of things, but what are the things themselves, they cannot*
> *tell. The materialist insists on facts, on history, on the force of*
> *circumstances, and the animal wants of man; the idealist on*
> *the power of Thought and of Will, on inspiration, on miracle,*
> *on individual culture.*

We are fully aware how successfully Materialism has come to
dominate the philosophical and scientific landscape. In its envi-
ronment, religion sits outside the material realm and becomes
something "other," a faith system with numerous cultural traditions firmly attached. In this system, materialism is defined
as reality and religion lies outside as some other reality or not
connected to reality at all.

Idealism, on the other hand, barely hangs on as a philosophy,
even though its roots go further back before Emerson into early
history before materialism. It is steeped in what we sometimes
call the wisdom traditions, including the Perennial Philosophy

and Neoplatonism, to name two significant traditions. The important principle here, however, is that Idealism claims to be the one reality as opposed to materialism. It is not "other" but rather contains the tangible world as part of its reality.

At present, Materialism, along with Secular Humanism, dominate both philosophy and science. As Emerson framed it, the materialist trusts the data of the senses, including of course the instruments which expand the range of the senses, such as telescopes, microscopes, radio telescopes, and particle accelerators. The problem is that these instruments are currently challenging the definitions of sensory empiricism we have accepted now for centuries.

In the materialist system, the mind is seen as an epiphenomenon of evolution. That is, the human brain (materialism's location of mind) evolved through time to its present capacity for conscious thought and reasoning. Materialism also posits that most of our brain function is unconscious or subconscious, both of which we are generally not aware. Some analysis even suggests that we are aware of only five percent of brain function at any given moment.

Moreover, neuroscience has dominated publications and the media with research and findings that seek to explain the functioning of the brain. Amazon, for example, lists more than a thousand books currently in print on neuroscience and the brain, whereas Idealism as a philosophy accounts for half that many. Still, it is surprising to learn that Amazon currently lists more than five hundred books under Idealism and Philosophy.

To suggest that Idealism is making a comeback as a serious and relevant theory of reality after its heyday with the Emerson Circle is unrealistic, however, despite signs of continued life. Another difficulty is that the word *idealism* also suggests an attitude as well as a philosophy. In this more limited sense, an idealist is one who holds high ideals of conduct and who demands the same for public officials and persons in positions of authority and power.

It is true, however, that Emerson's definition of Idealism has been making some progress as a serious alternative to Material- ism ever since what we now call the New Physics has emerged from the inner sanctum of theoretical physics into the public domain. As I have written elsewhere and as many others have as well, the New Physics has made serious inroads into the territory of the materialist worldview. We are no longer so certain that matter behaves as we thought it did or that it is the substance we thought it was. New experiments in quantum mechanics call into question old definitions of matter and energy.[3]

One new book published in 2012, *How the Hippies Saved Physics* by David Kaiser, is an entertaining and substantive look at advances in understanding this new world of matter and energy. It also suggests a fundamental role for the human mind in defining reality itself, which is a key principle in Emerson's Idealism. As we shall see below, Emerson's key statement in "Natural History of Intellect" makes a similar point: "In all sciences the student is discovering that nature, as he calls it, is always working, in wholes and in every detail, after the laws of the mind." And then he states the principle more clearly: "Intellect builds the universe and is the key to all it contains." Emerson first introduced this principle poetically in *Nature*, but here it becomes a philosophic principle of reality.

2. NATURE AS MAYA.

As we saw in *Nature*, Emerson established a sequence of uses or characteristics that Nature reveals to us. In Chapter Six, entitled "Idealism," Emerson reveals his attachment to Eastern concepts of reality, referring to the principle of Maya, or illusion, as "the noble doubt." Hindu philosophy answers the mystery of the nature of reality by denying the evidence of the senses and, thus rising above sensory evidence, characterizing nature, the world we perceive, as illusion.

It was not until Einstein upset the Newtonian reality by equating matter and energy that the West could grasp what Hindu ancients had declared. Einstein simply said $E = m$, and because he needed a conversion factor, he squared the speed of light in ergs (hence c-squared) to balance the equation. All matter is convertible to energy, like the wax in a candle or the photons from the sun in nuclear fusion.

Gradually the world came to understand that the stability we always assumed to be the nature of a steady-state universe was dynamic, in motion, flux, and that state was impermanent. Some of the starlight we see in the night sky has come to us from billions of light years away and the star we think we see at that distance isn't there anymore. As one physicist put it, "There's no there, there," a phrase which turned out to be a good description of Maya.

If, as Emerson assumed, Maya is an accurate description of nature, then perhaps reality can be represented, analogized, as mind stuff. Indeed, it was Anaxagoras, the first philosopher to practice his art in classical Athens, who described mind in exactly those terms. He said, "Mind is infinite and self-ruling, and is mixed with no Thing, but is alone by itself." This theory had a huge impact on Greek philosophy just prior to Plato and afterward in Neoplatonism. That notion of Mind (or *Nous* in the Greek) gradually replaced the Olympian order and provided a rationale for non-religious speculation of an infinite order. In other words, Greek philosophy was Eastern Idealism moving West.

3. THE ANGLE OF VISION.

Emerson's argument in *Nature* was that Reason, with thought as its instrument, challenges the despotism of the senses to eventually show us the transparency of things and allows us to see the true nature of objects. Later, in the essays on mind, he advances on his subject to declare, "Every object in nature is a word to signify some fact in the mind." Now nature is subservient. If we perceive some object in nature that perplexes us and in which we see no meaning, we merely have to wait until it reveals itself as a fact in the mind. In other words, the mind is primary and not a secondary product of nature.

As Emerson sought to bring insight to listeners and readers, he moved his argument to more personal ground. In "Natural History of Intellect" he asked, "What is life but an angle of vision?" If we thought that we were to engage in a life of the mind, Emerson takes us out further and says that life itself is mind. Sitting and thinking is one thing, but it is quite another matter to see life itself as an angle of vision. He goes on in the same passage to the implications of this angle: "A man is measured by the angle at which he looks at objects." And if that won't serve, he shuts the door on the notion of contemplation as an art form or philosophy of life and asserts, "What is life but what a man thinks of all day?"

Life is thought, then, not action. We are to be measured finally by what we think about. Is it power, money, sex, achievement, talent, fame? Or perhaps life is anger, resentment, bitterness, revenge, martyrdom, fantasy, duty, sacrifice, idealism, compassion. As Hamlet understood, and Emerson explains, there is more in heaven and earth than is dreamt of in our ordinary philosophies.

4. THE VIRUS OF IDEALISM.

The final principle of Emerson's vision of Idealism is its impossibility, not in its being the truth of reality or not, but in grasping its essential mystery. On one hand, we are wholly and fully one with the universe because we are made of star stuff in the explosions of supernovas; but on the other, we also feel alone, individual, and very finite. Emerson tells us that the safety measures of the operating room are no defense against this virus. We approach the subject perilously because "the substance with which we deal is of that subtle and active quality that it intoxicates all who approach it."

If we ask ourselves on what grounds Emerson uses such extreme analogies to attach to Idealism, all we need do is look at his own personal struggles over a lifetime of conviction and articulation. At the start of his career as a Unitarian minister, he had security, reputation, social standing, and a bright future. He gave all those external advantages in the name of finding the truth of reality. We can say that had he not done so, we would never have known his name; but the price he paid was high and still there are those who dismiss him as a dreamer and fanatic.

Although it may feel safer to stay on the firm ground of the material world, what Emerson seems to want for us is to set aside the breathing, touching, and warming world for what he calls mere anecdotes of the intellect, "a sort of Farmer's Almanac of mental moods," he says. Really? we ask. Is that all we are promised? Is there not more? He replies, "I confine my ambition to true reporting . . . though I should get only one new fact in a year." What we may learn is that Emerson's version of "true reporting" is worth the attention and time that the one new fact reveals to us.

The Journey Begins

Emerson's engagement with the principles of Idealism did not begin with study in any traditional sense. It certainly did not come from his formal education at Harvard College, which by 1817, when he entered at age fourteen, was going through its own development under the influence of German Enlightenment scholarship. By 1823, two years out of college, uncertain of his future, engaged temporarily as a schoolteacher, and barely older than his students, he opened the journal in which he had been writing for four years and wrote a remarkable declaration of faith and personal conviction: It could not have come from a source other than his own instinctive resources.

> *Who is he that shall control me? Why may not I act & speak & think with entire freedom? What am I to the universe, or, the Universe, what is it to me? Who hath forged the chains of Wrong & Right, of Opinion and Custom? And must I wear them? Is society my anointed King? Or is there any mightier community or any man or more than man, whose slave I am? I am solitary in the vast society of beings; I consort with no species; I indulge no sympathies. I see the world, human, brute & inanimate nature; I am in the midst of them, but not of*

them; I hear the sound of the storm,—the Winds & warring Elements sweep by me—but they mix not with my being. I see cities & nations & witness passions,—the roar of their laughter,—but I partake it not;—the yell of their grief,—it touches no chord in me; their fellowships & fashions, lusts and virtues, the words & deeds they call glory and shame,—I disclaim them all. I say to the Universe, Mighty one! thou art not my mother; Return to chaos, if thou wilt, I shall still exist. I live. If I owe my being, it is to a destiny greater than thine. Star by Star, world by world, system by system shall be crushed,—but I shall live. (JMN, V.I, December 21, 1823)

We may be tempted to say that this is a traditional declaration of faith in an immortal soul, but the language reveals a more ancient, even primitive, source than Judeo-Christian imagery. I am reminded again of Anaxagoras and his description of *Nous*, or Mind, as a separate and independent substance from ordinary matter. Richardson describes the passage as "a feeling of absolute and unquestioned self-validation, an extraordinary self-assertion, a wild romantic cogito that answers Hume not by logical argument but by felt experience."[4]

Here, then, we can say is the first of Emerson's "one new fact in a year" of reporting. Richardson's reference to David Hume (1711–1776) underscores Emerson's rebellion from his formal education, reacting to Hume's skeptical treatment of any claim of personal revelation. The young Emerson's final assertion—"If I owe my being, it is to a destiny greater than thine"—became for him at the same time an affirmation and a mystery. In the next ten years he would confront a harrowing and yet exhilarating series of events that would challenge his conviction as to where he truly owed his being.

Between 1823 and 1831, Emerson studied at Harvard's Divinity College; was ordained a Unitarian minister; met and

married the young and beautiful Ellen Tucker, who soon suc-
cumbed to tuberculosis; resigned his ministerial post; sold all his
worldly goods; traveled to Europe where he met Wordsworth,
Coleridge, and Carlyle; and returned to America and settled in
Concord, Massachusetts and began writing *Nature*.

My conflation of this decade of Emerson's life is meant to
reflect the intensity of the life-changing events he experienced. It
also illustrates the strength of his Idealist declaration of destiny
made in 1823, at the age of only twenty. Each of the events of
those years taken as an isolated experience has produced many
pages in his biographical record. And yet through it all is this
affirmation to "disclaim them all" in favor of a destiny increasingly ruled, as we shall see, by the power of an expansive mind.

When Emerson published *Essays I* in 1841 he began the
series with this sentence in "History": "There is one mind common to all individual men." It was a clarion call for the first
principle of Idealism. The principle, however, was muted by
the imagery and tone of subsequent essays in the series, which
tended toward human experience in the context of the more
universal principle of mind. Look for example at this passage
from "History" and see how the shift takes place:

> *Of the universal mind each individual man is one more incar-*
> *nation. All its properties consist in him. Each new fact in his*
> *private experience flashes a light on what great bodies of men*
> *have done, and the crises of his life refer to national crises.*
> *Every revolution was first a thought in one man's mind, and*
> *when the same thought occurs to another man, it is the key to*
> *that era. Every reform was once a private opinion, and when*
> *it shall be a private opinion again, it will solve the problem*
> *of the age.*

When Emerson writes in "History," "The universal nature,

too strong for the petty nature of the bard, sits on his neck and writes through his hand," our attention is drawn to the notion of inspiration and the creative muse and less to the nature of the universal nature we might wish to explore further.

In the twentieth century, Freud and Jung in particular presented us with the role of the unconscious and subconscious aspects of mind. Jung took the notion of a universal mind and gave it the name of the collective unconscious, thus planetizing its universal nature and reducing it to evolutionary collective memory. The resulting reductionism took center stage and it was not until the reflections of the quantum physicists restored mind to its universal or cosmic character.

It is not until "The Over-Soul" that universal mind emerges as a concept to be examined in greater depth. Emerson's choice of the term "over-soul," however, has tended to make the concept diffuse, especially when Emerson also uses terms like Supreme Critic, One, Highest Law, and Unity to broaden its character. Later, he refers also to pure nature and sovereign nature as well; nor does he neglect God while finally closing by simply using "soul."

Emerson closes "The Over-Soul" with an over-arching sentiment that the world is "the perennial miracle which the soul worketh." As a concluding sentiment, however, it leaves us uncertain about the relation of the over-soul to our own self-reliant lives and to our own spiritual journeys. What finally is our relation to this greater mind and what is its nature?

Essays, Second Series was originally published in 1844, three years after *Essays, First Series.* The major event in Emerson's life during this period was the death of his son Waldo Jr., aged five, who died quite suddenly in 1842 from scarlet fever. The essay "Experience" reflects upon this tragic event and is thought by many to signal a turning point in Emerson's vision. The late

Barbara Packer's *Emerson's Fall,* explores what Packer called the "opacity of human perception."[5] This view is substantial now among academic Emerson scholars.

This middle period of Emerson's creative life laid stress on the human condition, and its centerpiece is the essay "Experience." Here is the beginning of the essay, laying out its theme:

> *Where do we find ourselves? In a series of which we do not know the extremes, and believe that it has none. We wake and find ourselves on a stair; there are stairs below us, which we seem to have ascended; there are stairs above us, many a one, which go upward and out of sight. But the Genius which, according to the old belief, stands at the door by which we enter, and gives us the lethe to drink, that we may tell no tales, mixed the cup too strongly, and we cannot shake off the lethargy now at noonday. Sleep lingers all our lifetime about our eyes, as night hovers all day in the boughs of the fir-tree. All things swim and glitter. Our life is not so much threatened as our perception.*

As it is plain to see, the greater mind is not only silent here but absent. Emerson returns to the tradition of Judeo-Christian imagery: "It is very unhappy, but too late to be helped, the discovery we have made, that we exist. That discovery is called the Fall of Man." As the essay develops we look for that Over-Soul, Supreme Critic, or universal mind to emerge, but the essay concludes with a disheartening sense that the greater mind will not reveal itself. "But I have not found that much was gained by manipular attempts to realize the world of thought."

What sustained Emerson through this period was his attention and devotion to the thought of Plato and the Neoplatonists, particularly Plotinus and Proclus. Always present in his mind was a vision of the structure of the cosmos defined by Plato in the "Timaeus" and then refined by Plotinus in his Enneads.

4:

The Neoplatonic Vision

We know that Emerson studied Plato and Plotinus through
the filter of the Thomas Taylor translations. Taylor was a self-
taught classical scholar, friend of William Blake, and supported
in his work by a series of wealthy patrons, most notably William
Meredith, businessman and lover of the arts. Taylor's English
translations of Plato and Plotinus reached the Emerson group
early on in the earliest days of Transcendentalism. Fortunately
for scholars we have detailed records of Emerson's use of this
material.

Taylor was an Idealist who formed his thought through Neoplatonism. It is evident in his translations that his interpretation
of the thought of the Neoplatonists so infused his mind and
heart that the final English syntax he chose reflected that interpretation and created a subjective whole. Emerson became aware
in later years of Taylor's bias, with the result that he tempered
his enthusiasm and yet also remained a Taylor advocate if not
a disciple.

For our purposes, therefore, I have chosen to include here
some excerpts from Taylor's personal creed, which comes to us
from his essay entitled "The Platonic Philosopher's Creed."[6]
(See Appendix II.). We see in Emerson's text of "Natural His-

tory of Intellect" a similar pattern of affirmation as in Taylor's creed. Of course, creeds traditionally begin with "I believe . . ." but in this case the similarities suggest overt influence. Taylor's first principle sets the stage:

1. I BELIEVE in one first cause of all things, whose nature is so immensely transcendent, that it is even super-essential; and that in consequence of this it cannot properly either be named, or spoken of, or conceived by opinion, or be known, or perceived by any being.

Taylor developed the nature of mystery and impenetrability of the One or Absolute in subsequent references, following Plotinus in doing so. Emerson also began his lecture series with a similar statement:

I believe in the existence of the material world as the expression of the spiritual or the real, and in the impenetrable mystery which hides (and hides by absolute transparency) the mental nature. I await the insight which our advancing knowledge of material laws shall furnish.

Emerson introduces a paradox into his creed by suggesting that the impenetrable nature of the first cause "hides by absolute transparency." His own experience showed him the truth of this paradox when as a young man he had what came to be known as the 'transparent eye-ball' experience. As he described it at the time, he said, "I am nothing, I see all." The transparency, then, took place with the withdrawal of the ego, a letting-go and giving-in to the revelation.

Hiding through transparency also suggests invisibility and reminds us of a conversation Emerson had with a traditionally religious colleague who remarked that if something was not so in this world it would be in the "other world," to which Emerson

replied, "Other world? There is no other world." We have to sup-
pose, then, that transparency serves to mask the spiritual realm,
with its powers, entities, forces operating within it. Presupposing
a world which contains all material and spiritual elements does
solve the problem of considering the childish notion of heaven
in the clouds somewhere.

Thomas Taylor may have also suggested to Emerson an
important distinction between philosophical and scientific principles, a distinction which Emerson faced when he visited the
Jardin des Plantes in Paris in 1833. He had been so taken with
the scientific display of animals, organs, and skeletons that he
wrote in his journal, "I will be a naturalist," a vow he kept at least
in his reading and major areas of interest, if not in profession.

But Taylor, in his Introduction to the works of Plotinus, had
said, "The mathematical sciences are indeed the proper means
of acquiring wisdom, but they ought never to be considered
its end." Emerson would take this advice seriously, remaining
fully philosophical in his work while exploring science, including mathematics, in his reading. As we shall see, this principle
and interest will help us to carry out Emerson's devotion to the
truth of Idealism as mathematics becomes the new power in
the study of reality.

It becomes clear in Taylor's translations of Plotinus that Intellect is more than a mental faculty; it is an entity. In his essay
"On Intellect, Ideas, and (Real) Being" Plotinus (with help from
Taylor) explores the nature of Intellect and what it may mean to
capitalize the term. The argument goes that Intellect is indeed
a being, and as such it is separate from the Soul, just as Anaxagoras saw Mind separate from All Things (*ta panta*). Intellect
emanates from the highest (the Good) down to those mortal
beings who are capable of receiving its emanations.

These transmissions can take the form of concepts which in

turn are transmuted in human beings to scientific formulations and theories and hence, if they are accurate, to mathematical expressions, or equations. This Plotinic formulation becomes a Neoplatonic equivalent of the inspiration of genius and scientific "discovery." Some scientists have understood this principle and refer to their so-called discoveries as "uncoveries," meaning they merely uncovered or revealed what was always transparently "hiding" in plain sight.

If, as we assume, Emerson was imbued with this notion of Intellect, we can more fully understand how he can elevate Intellect into its elevated position in his hierarchy of mental attributes. It also suggests to us how Emerson was able to express the notion that Intellect is not in us as much as we are in it. The Neoplatonic Intellect pervades all of reality and can help us understand Emerson when he says, "I believe in the existence of the material world as the expression of the spiritual or the real . . . [which] hides by absolute transparency." Once seen, Emerson says, "the oracle will need no priest."

Maturity and Theories of Mind

As the 1840s drew to a close, Emerson was focused on his lecture career. He spent much of 1845 and the next three years on what would become in book form *Representative Men,* his celebration of the world's greatest thinkers, writers, and statesmen. For publication he wrote an introduction entitled "Uses of Great Men," and in it he returned to a consideration of the nature of mind. Emerson speculates on the nature of great men, what allows genius to burst forth, and how invention and discovery actually take place. He writes, "In the history of discovery, the ripe and latent truth seems to have fashioned a brain for itself. A magnet must be made man in some Gilbert, or Swedenborg, or Oerstad, before the general mind can come to entertain its powers."

Here, perhaps for the first time, for Emerson at least, a pattern emerges in the hierarchy of mind. We get a glimpse of how things work. A ripe and latent truth—that is, a moment when some mystery of nature is ready to be revealed as a truth, a theory made manifest—prepares, or fashions, a brain in an individual from which the truth will emerge. An attraction from the greater mind congeals into a mathematical equation, an insight, a formulation in words or design, in other words "made man" so that the higher mind or inspiration can transmit.

Our best examples of this process are Maxwell's laws of electromagnetism and Einstein's theories of relativity. Philosophers of science have marveled at the way in which the human mind is able to formulate fundamental laws of the universe and express them into abstracted expressions like $E = mc^2$, seemingly so simple an expression but so comprehensive a fundamental truth.

Even Maxwell confessed that what he expressed in his fundamental laws came from what he said was beyond his own knowledge and understanding. The expression "the general mind can come to entertain its powers," is very close to how many great scientists describe the moment of discovery. We think it is merely humility, whereas it is probably the exact way in which truth manifests. Emerson puts the matter this way:

> *The high functions of the intellect are so allied that some imaginative power usually appears in all eminent minds, even in arithmeticians of the first class, but especially in meditative men of an intuitive habit of thought. This class serve us, so that they have the perception of identity and the perception of reaction. The eyes of Plato, Shakespeare, Swedenborg, Goethe, never shut on either of these laws. The perception of these laws is a kind of metre of the mind.*

The reason that Emerson's formulation has merit has emerged in various discussions of why and how the human brain is capable of formulating universal laws that seem to have very little practical use in human culture or society. As one biologist expressed it, knowing the laws of relativity has very little evolutionary advantage for a human being. Why bother?

One answer is of course intense curiosity, the desire to know, which Aristotle stated is fundamental to humans. Emerson's more complex answer has more to do with the nature of mind itself, the full range of hierarchy which begins at the lowest level with physical instinct and at the highest with universal values revealed because the highest mind wants them revealed.

In "The Over-Soul" Emerson used the word Unity as a synonym for universal mind, reminding us that the universe, earth, and all life is One, and because human beings have the capacity to absorb this diversity into a unity, we become, at least in terms of perception, the center of this unity. Emerson's powers of eloquence and observation express this unity:

> *A man is a centre for nature, running out threads of relation through every thing, fluid and solid, material and elemental. The earth rolls; every clod and stone comes to the meridian: so every organ, function, acid, crystal, grain of dust, has its relation to the brain. It waits long, but its turn comes.*

Regardless of periods of discouragement and shifts of direction, Emerson maintained his devotion to universal mind throughout his long career, which spanned nearly forty years of lecturing and as much in writing. As he approached the 1850s, he began to return to a deeper consideration of the nature of mind in a series of six lectures entitled "Natural Method of Mental Philosophy." Some of the content from these lectures found its way into the Harvard Lectures in 1871–1872 and then was published after his death as "Natural History of Intellect."

Using the imagery of nature, from which all reality traces its origins, Emerson analogizes the relation of the human to the universal mind by describing how the planets are formed from the exhalations of the sun.

> *It is a steep stair down from the essence of Intellect pure to thoughts and intellections. As the sun is conceived to have*

made our system by hurling out from itself the outer rings of
diffuse ether which slowly condensed into earths and moons, by
a higher force of the same law the mind detaches minds, and a
mind detaches thoughts or intellections. These again all mimic in
their sphericity the first mind, and share its power.

The steep step down from pure thought to human intellections is more like a cliff, or to use an earlier image, to rise from intellection to pure thought is like swimming up Niagara Falls, just as it would be impossible for the sun to withdraw its solar system back to itself. The analogy also has a more valuable point about the nature of revelation. He warned against those who claimed to have received personal messages from higher realms. He called it fanaticism. Human history seems to have proved him right.

In a decisive shift, it is during this period that Emerson began using the term Intellect to correspond to both human and universal mind. Since the word 'mind' contains every aspect of mental functioning, including dreams, awareness, consciousness, unconsciousness, reason, fantasy, daydreams, calculation, and imagination, the term Intellect (capitalized) became the focus of his inquiry. He wanted to connect higher to lower Intellect and to measure its depth.

The word 'Reason' had close and similar meaning, but Intellect expressed a purer sense. Using Intellect, Emerson could refer to the word 'intellectual' as belonging to a person engaged in higher modes of thought, as well as one capable of connecting the worlds of knowledge and understanding through conscious thought and intuition.

PART II
The Harvard Lectures or Natural History of Intellect

IT MAY WELL BE A MISNOMER to call what follows the
Harvard Lectures. The structure of "Natural History of Intellect"
is broken and difficult to summarize. The attempt which follows
is designed to highlight main topics and to offer a personal frame
for the material. It is clear, however, that the attempt may well
further misrepresent what the extended essay (more than twice
the length of Emerson's usual essay length) offers to us as what
Emerson actually presented to the tiny group of listeners who
attended.

Perhaps the better part of wisdom is to say that what follows
is a commentary on the essay and not an attempt to structure
actual lectures. The published version assembled by Emerson's
friend and editor James Cabot can be described as follows:

I. The Powers and Laws of Thought
    Three brief sections on the nature of Intellect, its rela-
    tion to Nature, and an introduction to Instinct and
    Inspiration (approximately twenty-eight pages)

II. Instinct and Inspiration
    With an emphasis on the sources of our mental powers

III. Memory
    Memory as the matrix of human faculties

Suffice to say, we will find considerable overlapping of
content with regard to the central theses of Intellect, Instinct,

Inspiration, Genius, and Memory. In his biography *The Life of Emerson,* Van Wyck Brooks described the state of things as Emerson wrestled with this assignment, ". . . his hands fumbled with the manuscript, as he turned over a dozen pages, turned back another dozen, skipped, let pages fall onto the floor—who cared for order or system in these thoughts?"[7]

Notwithstanding what seems like presentational chaos, the work which remains serves our purpose quite well.

1:

The Powers and Laws
of Thought

Emerson's comment earlier about genuine seekers needing no
priest appeared at the beginning of his Harvard Lectures in his
creed. He told the students that they "shall come to know that
in seeing and in no tradition [they] must find what truth is."8 In
his much postponed return to Harvard he affirmed his thesis in
the Divinity School Address that the truth of reality would not
be revealed in any religious tradition. But in this lecture room,
no faculty sat in judgment of the assertion.

Emerson's individualism, his mistrust of "academies and uni-
versities," as he put it, must have shocked his students, if they
comprehended what he was saying. After all, there they were at
Harvard, sitting in a classroom, and here was this famous old
man telling them that their formal education would not reveal
the truth. If we think Emerson kind or patient in his opening remarks, consider the passage beginning "Seek the literary
circles . . ." and read it aloud. Your voice will rise, your mood
darken, and the effect will make you uneasy in your chair. (See
Appendix I)

Even the philosophers and prophets will not help, they being guilty of clouding the truth "by a strange confounding in [their] own mind of private folly with the public wisdom." And if the students should flee to society they will learn even less, where "they play the game of conversation, as they play billiards, for pastime and credit."

In other words, Emerson takes away all the ordinary avenues of study and knowledge we normally seek, even the world of practicality where we employ our talents to create and accomplish. Even here we cannot find what we are seeking, that is, if we are seeking at all. So, what is to be done? Where do we begin?

The teaching begins with one of Emerson's most important observations. "What is life but the angle of vision?" He reiterates it. "A man is measured by the angle at which he looks at objects." In other words, what we see depends on how we see. It cannot be otherwise. What Einstein discovered about the nature of the cosmos was a function of his unique angle of vision. He began with a series of thought problems. What would it be like, for example, to be a photon moving along on a beam of light?

Emerson also shocked his students by next asking them, "What is life but what a man is thinking about all day?" Did this question penetrate? Did he wake them from their private thoughts, their daydreaming? It must have been an effective means of attracting their attention, of bringing them into the moment. One wonders if he paused to consider this point or did he move along in his text?[9] In the next paragraph he did actually say, "Let me have your attention to this dangerous subject."

It is here that he asks, "Can you swim up Niagara Falls?" This is in the context of any serious attempt at introversion, to which, he says, "we have an invincible repugnance." He once wrote in a *Dial* essay, "Ask a man to study himself and he can think of nothing less interesting." The reason for this lack of interest is a lack of self-trust. We don't really think we are very interesting or that if we take the time, we will find anything valuable in our memory banks or thought processes. We have been trained away from such "navel-gazing" activity as though it is neurotic or even dangerous.

This sense of danger is the reason for Emerson's comment above. He tries to counter that reaction with these next paragraphs, preparing the field of inquiry with the reassurance that looking inward and preparing a profitable angle of vision would lead to greater knowledge and understanding.

And what is the nature of this inquiry? Metaphysics, which even today is regarded not so much as a dangerous subject but rather just an outmoded one. Philosophy has jettisoned metaphysics from the ship of inquiry as being both dangerous and just unwelcome. The reason is not so much that study of past metaphysics yields little of value, but more to the point that such inquiry cannot be trusted because observations coming from such inquiry are merely opinion and cannot be proved true empirically. Emerson is out of mainstream fashion for this reason. But as he put it in "Experience," "Never mind the ridicule, never mind the defeat: up again, old heart!"

Emerson's answer to those who negate the findings of metaphysical speculation is stated right here: "Metaphysics must be perpetually reinforced by life, must be the observations of a working-man on working-men; must be biography." The ivory tower won't reveal truth. We have to have our feet on the ground, in nature, working with nature, on nature, for nature. I can trust a man who can say, as Emerson did, "There are only twenty minutes in the life of a pear when it is fit to eat." It's true.

In other words, metaphysics must be practical and life-enhancing. His last and soaring instigation on the subject follows his critical analysis and warnings:

My metaphysics are to the end of use. I wish to know the laws
of this wonderful power, that I may domesticate it. I observe
with curiosity its risings and settings, illumination and eclipse;
its obstructions and its provocations, that I may learn to live
with it wisely, court its aid, catch sight of its splendor, feel its
approach, hear and save its oracles and obey them.

At this point in his introductory appeal, Emerson lays out
the structure of this first part of the series, entitled "Powers and
Laws of Thought:"

First, I wish to speak of the excellence of that element, and
the great auguries that come from it, notwithstanding the
impediments which our sensual civilization puts in the way.

Next, I treat of the identity of the thought with Nature; and
I add a rude list of some by-laws of the mind.

Thirdly, I proceed to the fountains of thought in Instinct and
Inspiration, and I also attempt to show the relation of men of
thought to the existing religion and civility of the present time.

I. THE NATURE OF INTELLECT

Rather than begin by defining Intellect as Plotinus (or his sur-
rogate Taylor) might, Emerson poeticizes Intellect as an ethereal
sea, fathomless, infinite and yet part of nature, to be imagined
and perhaps even understood. The key to its relation to human
thought is the wonder and awe it inspires, and it is this wonder
that allows us to approach it. "To Be is the unsolved, unsolvable
wonder." Imagine how those alive in 1871 thought of the sea:
two-thirds of the earth's surface, unexplored, too deep to fathom,
too powerful to contain or conquer.

The next image is of the river, connected to thought, so

that we see clearly the relation between the sea of Intellect and the river of thought: those same waters, the same fundamental nature but one infinite in scope but also the means of our navigation in the world. Emerson connects the two by making the observation that possibly the river not only makes its own banks, but is "makes perhaps the observer, too."

This hint that the human instrument we call mind has the capacity to migrate or transform itself into a self-reflective instrument, one which gives us the ability to observe the observer, or as the psychologist once asked, "Who is the dreamer who dreams the dream?"[10]

Once Emerson sets this particular stage, he returns to his creed in order to let the students know the source of his metaphysical position, which of course is Idealism:

I am of the oldest religion. Leaving aside the question which was prior, egg or bird, I believe the mind is the creator of the world, and is ever creating;—that at last Matter is dead Mind; that mind makes the senses it sees with; that the genius of man is a continuation of the power that made him and that has not done making him.

We see the Idealist position (or religion as Emerson says) in the statement that *the mind makes the senses it sees with.* This statement is as clear a contrast to Materialism as can be expressed. Either Mind is the source, the truth of reality, or it is not. If not, then matter is fundamental and mind is epiphenomenal.

Continuing with the relationship between Intellect and thought, Emerson reiterates the deep chasm between the two by saying, "It is a steep stair down from the essence of Intellect pure to thoughts and intellections." And here, by example, is the reference we saw made earlier to the sun (as Intellect) hurling its essence out to make the solar system, nature, and us

(Thought and intellections). The relation of Intellect to thought is described as sphericity (as the sun is a sphere so are the planets and moons). It is a neat analogy.

II. THE IDENTITY OF THOUGHT WITH NATURE

If we wonder how it is that the human mind is capable of discovering the laws of nature, all we need realize is that the mind we use to make these discoveries is structured just as nature is. The mind knows its own nature and gives that nature to us in our ability to express its laws. The reason we make errors in exploring nature is that the framework we are given through tradition or education is itself in error, but when we finally make the correct discovery we see it so clearly we wonder how we could have gotten it so wrong for so long. Therefore the first step in study is to trust the relation between our mind and the object in nature we seek to know. A side benefit to this process is that we are then able to reverse the process and learn the laws of the mind through the study of nature.

Emerson puts the matter this way: "From whatever side we look at Nature we seem to be exploring the figure of a disguised man." Why disguised? It is because we do not see clearly and the mind within the person remains in the shadows until we learn how to shine light on the whole to find the unity. The references made by Emerson through this section remind us of the experience of watching the Olympic games or any great athletic competition, to see and to feel the laws of the body being articulated and displayed with such clarity and detail. The evidence shows that people watching are often inspired to emulate what they see, or at least to make the attempt.

If the example of other persons is not followed, Emerson points to plant life, in the germination, growth, and various changes and crises of vegetable life. The examples point to an awakening of the mind, when it is "surcharged . . . with thoughts in which it delights and . . . becomes active." But then there arises another paradox. "The moment a man begins not to be convinced, that moment he begins to convince."

The mind awakens in the questioning mode to begin questing. If we are convinced by the first observation we hear, the mind is not awakened; it accepts passively and remains in that passive mode of learning. Not being convinced, on the other hand, I awaken. Such is the truth of this principle, Emerson says, that "in unfit company the finest powers are paralyzed." We seldom realize in the normal course of events the importance of good company to the health and growth of the mind. That fact is why Emerson emphasized "the escape from all false ties" as the first principle of the self-reliant life. (See the final paragraph of "Considerations by the Way" from *Conduct of Life*.)

If we seek out or merely find ourselves by good fortune in good company, we become capable of receiving wisdom from that company. The ancient Greeks tell us that wisdom is transcendental and unique, not in the company of the other virtues, which is why Athena, goddess of wisdom, is not born but bursts from the forehead of Zeus, Great Consciousness. This Greek sense of Mind (Nous) embodied in the figure of Zeus marks one of the characteristics of Hellenism, that period following the Classical within which Plato and his Academy began to modify the Olympian myth and to formulate instead a view of divinity closer to what would become Neoplatonism with Plotinus and eventually the West's vision of Idealism.

In like manner, Emerson's lectures at Harvard make a similar shift of focus following this reference to wisdom and its infusion into the minds of individuals who seek out good company.

An individual mind in like manner is a fixation or momentary eddy in which certain services and powers are taken up and minister in petty niches and localities, and then, being released, return to the unbounded soul of the world. In this eternal resurrection and rehabilitation of transitory persons, who and what are they? 'Tis only the source that we can see;—the eternal mind, careless of its channels, omnipotent in itself, and continually ejaculating its torrent into every artery and vein and veinlet of humanity. Wherever there is health, that is, consent to the cause and constitution of the universe, there is perception and power.

Following this outburst of affirmation, Emerson concentrates on the virtues of spiritual self-reliance as the one and only way in which we have access to the "eternal mind." He does this in short bursts (ejaculations as he says) of principle:

Each man is a new power in nature. But he enters the world by one key.

Every man is a new method and distributes things anew. Absolutely speaking, I can only work for myself.

The one thing not to be forgiven to intellectual persons is that they believe in the ideas of others.

Emerson's profound and fundamental independence demands a conscious, self-reflective awareness of influence. Those who join organizations or communal groups where so-called leaders inject thoughts and ideas for the purposes of control and manipulation lose themselves, perhaps forever. The definition of a cult is just this kind of manipulation of thought and idea. It is a prison in which independent thought is discouraged and respect for such thought is absent.

In our highly charged partisan climate, we don't have to be a member of such a cult or organization to feel this kind of pressure. The inundation of media, advertising, and electronic communication of all kinds invites and intrudes on our thoughts, seeking to influence, if not control, our lives. Some believe our government is also guilty of this practice, hence the paranoia of members of the Tea Party and all anti-government rhetoric.

Schools and education in general influence our thinking permanently only if we abdicate our own individual sovereignty. Emerson points out in many places that children naturally learn the language and accents of their parents, but at some point find their own thought and expression. If they do not, they are lost. Such loss is one of the great tragedies of life.

It might also be mentioned that if a child grows up in an intellectual family, there is greater influence on thoughts and ideas and greater need for developing independence. We often see in the natural rebellion of adolescence tendencies of rejection from an intellectual tradition, as children find their own way; but also, they may choose, out of instinctive rebellion, the opposite set of ideas rather than intellectual independence.

One of the virtues of Idealism is its neutrality in matters of influence. As Emerson points out, nature is mute. It offers no opinions and no dogma, no rules to follow except common sense and the laws of necessity. Its wisdom is also neutral, allowing us the freedom to think as we will. Emerson's essay "Compensation" is an excellent source of nature's wisdom. And as he says in the next section, section three, "The healthy mind lies parallel to the currents of nature and sees things in place, or makes discoveries."

III. THE SOURCES OF MENTAL POWER

Emerson's Idealism has two sources of genius or mental power: Instinct and Inspiration. Both arise from our direct connection with nature, that is, that state or condition without interference from the ideas of others.

In Idealism, instinct is a natural intuitive power. In Emerson, instinct is also equivalent to wit. Alexander Pope said, "True Wit is Nature to advantage dress'd/ What oft was thought but ne'er so well express'd;/Something whose truth convinced at sight we find,/ That gives us back the image of our mind."[11]

Pope's use of the word "advantage" suggests an advantage to us, to human beings, able to see and understand the laws of nature through the exercise of "true wit." Emerson's interpretation is similar to Pope's. It means intelligence combined with natural insight unencumbered.

Instinct is our name for the potential wit. Each man has a feeling that what is done anywhere is done by the same wit as his. All men are his representatives, and he is glad to see that his wit can work at this or that problem as it ought to be done, and better than he could do it. We feel as if one man wrote all the books, painted, built, in dark ages; and we are sure that it can do more than ever was done. It was the same mind that built the world. That is Instinct.

We say, "She had an instinct for finding the right way." We also "follow our nose." At higher levels, where it comes to laws of nature or theories of the universe, our instincts may tell us that something we have learned is wrong or missing, but we may not trust what we feel because we assume we lack information. But later, our instinct may be proven right. It is a matter of self-trust.

The next step in the powers of instinct is inspiration, what Emerson wisely calls the power of instinct excited, or instinct "breaking its silence." Faced with mystery and the unknown, the instinct erupts and an inspiration surfaces like magma from a volcano. And like that eruption, it is the magma that makes new land and surfaces on which we can live and grow.

We are always intrigued as well as entertained when an intelligent observer offers an interpretation of ancient myth to shed light on its inner meanings. Emerson performs this sleight of hand in describing the Greek myth of Pan as an account of the moment when nature "first becomes intelligent."

> *The mythology cleaves close to nature; and what else was it they represented in Pan, god of shepherds, who was not yet completely finished in god-like form, blocked rather, and wanting the extremities; had emblematic horns and feet? Pan, that is, All. His habit was to dwell in mountains, lying on the ground, tooting like a cricket in the sun, refusing to speak, clinging to his behemoth ways. He could intoxicate by the strain of his shepherd's pipe,—silent yet to most, for his pipes make the music of the spheres, which because it sounds eternally is not heard at all by the dull, but only by the mind. He wears a coat of leopard spots or stars. He could terrify by earth-born fears called panics. Yet was he in the secret of nature and could look both before and after. He was only seen under disguises, and was not represented by any outward image; a terror sometimes, at others a placid omnipotence.*

We are reminded here of the previous reference to nature as a disguised man, again a firm connection to our natural heritage, fallen, a god in ruins, as he said, but still with a memory of our original form and its potential for self-recovery. Part of that process of recovery was the ability to transcend those earth-born fears or panics and to acquire that transcending nature to look both before and after. Such was the Greek instinct elevated to inspiration.

Once tamed, the primitive instinct elevated by the passion of inspiration becomes Perception, the eye of a more mature grasp of nature. And since, as Emerson says, "the senses minister to a mind they do not know," the mind has to order the incoming flow of data into rationality, aided by Reason. The result, he says, is that through this ordering process, which the Greeks attributed to Apollo, "we become aware of spiritual facts, of rights, of duties, of thoughts—a thousand faces of one essence. . . . and we call the essence Truth."

The next topic details the process of intellectual detachment. This description of detachment came to Emerson from his devotion to the Bhagavad Gita, an English translation of which he kept by his side for many years. Its central admonition to develop detachment is a mature and challenging spiritual task, one requiring discipline, attention, will, and self-control. The key, Emerson tells us, is to see the task of detachment in a universal light, not in the limiting temporal darkness.

Going out of ourselves, as Emerson phrases it, represents a higher act of will than mere self-awareness. It places our being in the possession of the witness or one who observes without engagement. In such a state we are able to act with dispassionate calm in order to do what must be done and done well. It is a state in which the fraud that is the ego no longer runs the show.

The ego's calling card is, "I did it!" If we call on the ego to take control, we slip into a world of illusion and self-deception, a world in which instinct, inspiration, and perception never appear, or if they seem to appear, it is because ego has absconded with their effects for its own illusory ends. What Emerson describes in this section is devoid of ego altogether. If the language seems unfamiliar, it is because of the absence of ego-language in the telling.

It is evident in this language and formulation of the principles of Idealism that the position of Intellect in the human realm or system guarantees that ego cannot be a presence there. If Intellect is universal, that is a presence or force outside the human mind but connected to it (Emerson uses the word "copula" to designate that connection); what modern psychology designates the ego has no place or power in it. The mind then considers Intellect the reigning influence and perception, together with instinct and discrimination it examines and confirms the inspiration.

Emerson identifies Genius as the gift of placing Intellect at the heart of one's mental life, and refers to it as "a delicate sensibility to the laws of the world." He means by this definition nature's laws as well as the higher or spiritual laws. In an individual, genius demonstrates its presence or power by the product of a new form in nature.

Our most dramatic example of genius remains Einstein, whose insights perceived a completely different form of space and time, resulting in space/time and which found its expression in a series of formulae, what Emerson referred to as insight "passing into realization." After all, Einstein did not change reality or create a new reality. He gave us the insight and then the means to understand the laws of the universe in a new and more accurate light. His work was followed by the new world of quantum mechanics, which truly did change the world.

If then we move from scientific discovery through genius to spiritual insight, we arrive at prophets, avatars, and visionaries from all ages. It is of these people Emerson speaks when he says, "that certain persons add to the common vision a certain degree of control over these states of mind." However, he notes, the perspective that is required to receive these hints from the great Mind also creates a break from unity because of the detachment required and that break severs the human instrument from the eternal source, leaving us adrift. This break from unity defines the human condition, making us even more grateful for momentary hints from that unity.

This observation from one who experienced these insights

comes with a severe warning that some genius is warped by the grace of perception and becomes self-involved and perverse, creating a false prophet, a person bloated with self-importance and egoistic tendencies. Such people are not difficult to recognize because they claim personal revelation by name, place, and time, all facts of life that never come to us through genuine revelation.

Emerson was extremely careful about discussing these rare moments of infusions from Intellect. We see in "Spiritual Laws" admonitions to be wary of false signs. Even in "Self-Reliance" he mentions being warned not to trust these intuitive inner thoughts. His response strikes us as extreme but its intent was to shock.

> *I remember an answer which when quite young I was prompted to make to a valued adviser, who was wont to importune me with the dear old doctrines of the church. On my saying, What have I to do with the sacredness of traditions, if I live wholly from within? my friend suggested,— "But these impulses may be from below, not from above." I replied, "They do not seem to me to be such; but if I am the Devil's child, I will live then from the Devil." No law can be sacred to me but that of my nature.*

The lesson here is that trust in one's own thought is dangerous, and safeguards must always be in place. The first is the biblical admonition that we can tell the value of these insights by their fruits. If the practical application of thought shows wisdom, then the source is reliable. And the second measure is that wisdom is measured by "the intellectual perception of truth and the moral sentiment of right."

Was Emerson the Devil's child? Some think so, that is, those who trust only in tradition and the word from sacred texts. After all, he was branded a heretic by the "wise" elders of Harvard.

Emerson's response to these doubters was expressed in the very first words he ever published in the Introduction to *Nature*, where he asked two essential questions: "Why should not we also enjoy an original relation to the universe? Why should not we have a poetry and philosophy of insight and not of tradition, and a religion by revelation to us, and not the history of theirs?"

The lectures under discussion here are both a continuation and a culmination of answers to those two questions. Emerson understood when he answered his "valued adviser" that his rather flippant reply had to be answered seriously. The remainder of his published work devoted to revelation and relationship to divinity was a direct answer to that advisor's warning. And here, in this lecture to students he was ever mindful of his responsibility.

The examples he gives in this section on sources of mental power are useful, especially today when new sects, cults, New Age revelations, and doomsday predictions pervade the Internet and ask for our financial support and adherence.

The new sect stands for certain thoughts. We go to individual members for an exposition of them. Vain expectation. They are possessed by the ideas but do not possess them. One meets contemplative men who dwell in a certain feeling and delight which are intellectual but wholly above their expression. They cannot formulate. They impress those who know them by their loyalty to the truth they worship but cannot impart.

A personal example might help here. Years ago, when I was studying in California, a couple who lived next door to my little garden house invited me to attend a meeting of "their organization." When I asked them what it was about, they said that they were learning how to become "clear." Later I learned that this was the term used by members of the Church of Scientology.

But on this occasion, when I pressed the couple to explain the notion of becoming "clear," they were unable to make sense or to discuss their organization openly. We never spoke again. "The grasp is the main thing," Emerson says. Intelligence is part of the art of grasping an idea or subject, but also crucial is judgment and discrimination. In the presence of new ideas a modicum of scepticism is necessary, but when scepticism dominates character and creates a Sceptic, the person is lost to the intimations of truth.

Emerson ends this section of the discussion of sources by saying "I have spoken of Intellect constructive," of how the power of Intellect finds use and practical value to human life. He was always impatient of progress, complaining that his own powers were weak and that moments of insight were too rare. "The pace of Nature is so slow," he complains, "as if Nature had sprained her foot—and plenteous stopping at little stations."

His subject here is the value and necessity of this slow pace. "The Delphian prophetess, when the spirit possesses her, is herself a victim. The excess of individualism, when it is not corrected or subordinated to the Supreme Reason, makes that vice which we stigmatize as monotones, men of one idea." Here again is the warning to beware of the excesses of spiritual possession.

Supreme Reason enters the discussion here for the first time. Reason is not the same as Intellect. The Intellect Emerson celebrates is a pure emanation from Mind, an influx of the laws of the universe uninhibited. It is the constructive power, as he said. The Supreme Reason, we learn from *Nature*, is what "considered in relation to nature, we call Spirit." Intellect emanates from Spirit as a force, a power, which reveals itself in human life as Genius, whereas Reason is one of the faculties of Spirit. To be subordinated to Supreme Reason, then, means placing oneself within the influence of Spirit as a check on the excesses of individuality.

Emerson compares the processes of Nature as being like a "penurious rill," or a small miserly trickle of water, not enough, we think, to sustain life, but since Nature is immortal, she has plenty of time and is in no hurry. We find that as one faculty is enhanced, empowered, others are diminished. We see this in savants who master all the facts of history but cannot tie their shoes. Emerson's answer to these mysteries about how Nature operates is "She does as she pleases."

In the light of Nature's seemingly whimsical behavior, human beings take it upon themselves to create order so as to find meaning and coherence in their lives. Emerson's next theme is to frame this effort for the students and he does so first by urging them "to write out the spirit of [their lives] symmetrically." To do so, to arrange general reflection in their natural order" is genius and is accomplished by only a few.

To say it frankly, Emerson himself was not always able to accomplish this aim, as he was not hesitant to admit, hence his frustration with his efforts to bring his natural eloquence under the rule of symmetrical order. It is often the case that when we recall some great sentence from his work, we cannot remember from what essay it comes. It is safe to say, then, that his recommendation to the students came from personal frustration.

An example of a great sentence appearing as if from nowhere is "The air would rot without lightning." In its context here we see that the image illustrates the point that we need antagonisms and radical expression in order to stay fresh and vital. He even says that we need bigotry in order to clear the air and focus our attention on matters of humanity and justice.

In order to bring clarity to his discussion of genius and its role in our spiritual development, Emerson sets up a duality, in this case talent versus genius. Talent is a lower form of genius, what takes us successfully in and through the world. Too often he tells us, we seize upon talent and ride it through life without considering the higher potential of genius that lurks within waiting to be awakened. In effect genius is our soul, the place where Intellect resides waiting to be heard and felt.

Too often, in individuals of great talent, such as physical, musical, mathematical, artistic, or literary, the gifted person is overwhelmed by talent and ignores the deeper and more important aspect of being that is marked by Genius. "Wide is the gulf between genius and talent," Emerson says. He is severe in saying that those who live by talent "entertain us for a time, but at the second or third encounter we have nothing more to learn." The irony is, of course, that we often envy talent and long to develop our own to the high levels of fame, only to discover that fame holds little satisfaction or meaning in the long run. Finding our Genius is the more subtle and difficult task, and the results of its expression are lasting. At the close of this section (possibly a specific lecture), Emerson returns to the notion of Intellect and Ego, to conflict and resolution.

> *The height of culture, the highest behavior, consists in the identification of the Ego with the universe; so that when a man says I hope, I find, I think, he might properly say, The human race thinks or finds or hopes. And meantime he shall be able continually to keep sight of his biographical Ego,—I have a desk, I have an office, I am hungry, I had an ague,—as rhetoric or offset to his grand spiritual Ego, without impertinence, or ever confounding them.*

This clarity seems a while coming in the sense of allowing us to have a clear view of the conflict. So many themes and concepts are reported here. First, of course, is the difference between the egoist's I and Mine with the universal "the human race thinks." In between we see the biological ego of "I have a desk" as opposed to the Emerson dictum, "This body is the office where I work." The formulation of "I work" is natural and expressive of the mind at work, which is the proper "I." The evidence throughout Emerson's work illustrates the consistency with which he uses the universal rhetoric. An observant mind attuned to this difference can tell easily when a writer is working from a personal or universal Ego.

2

Instinct and Inspiration

Following the Emersonian example, this portion of commentary will highlight six connected themes that Emerson links to the sources and powers of Instinct and Inspiration, themes which also include Intellect, Nature, and Mind.

I. SHIFTING RHETORIC

We have observed throughout Emerson's publishing history from *Nature* to this material a striking shift from the poetic to the scientific. It is a shift paralleled in the nineteenth century from Romanticism to Materialism in both England and America. Emerson's meetings with Coleridge and Wordsworth in 1833 clearly mark the beginning of the end of the Romantic period in poetry, as both aged poets failed to impress Emerson. It was Carlyle the sceptic, the social radical, who impressed Emerson and who became a friend for life.

As Emerson formulated the Idealist vision, he changed the language of that vision as new developments in geology, biology, physics, and mechanics emerged. His friend Louis Agassiz, the Swiss-born Harvard professor of geology and paleontology, was a constant source of knowledge and inspiration after 1846, a period which coincides with Emerson's more scientific interests. What is useful for our purposes is the realization that a development in scientific knowledge and understanding of the laws of nature need not undermine the foundations of Idealism.

Indeed, after Emerson's death and the revelations of Einstein in Physics and the birth of Quantum Mechanics, Idealism received a fresh impulse from the breakdown in matter into pulses of energy and the queer, unrealistic behavior of subatomic particles. For the present work, however, it was enough that Emerson was able to keep abreast of progress in science without a loss of conviction in the Idealist vision of universal mind.

In this section of the lectures, Emerson makes it clear that his early affirmations of universal mind and the principles of Idealism remain unchanged with the years and the scientific discoveries of his age. He says, "All men are, in respect to this source of truth, on a certain footing of equality, equal in original science, though against appearance; and 't is incredible to them." Here he is turning Instinct into a resource for trust and patience. Instinct also tells us that what the senses tell us is appearance only, which early on we may see as truth but later, that same power reports a higher and finer physical and moral order.

II. INSPIRATION RISING FROM INSTINCT.

He reminds us, then, of the connection between Instinct and Inspiration, the latter being Instinct "put in action." Also, new knowledge is imparted here. Instinct, we learn, is mute, and needs to be excited into action by the wisdom of Inspiration. In effect Inspiration is the command "Let there be light" in the creation. The key is what he calls "some instigation, some impulse." It is an instigation which must be followed once perceived as a feeling or emotion. All inspiration comes to light as a feeling, an urge to speak out, to reach out into the world, to articulate from the ground of passion and love. What is rare, Emerson confides, is the completion of human inspiration into its proper form, the follow-through to completion. It is human nature to begin projects, but it is divine inspiration that completes the task. Spirit is an even, silent, and continuous power that sustains the human passion to create, to complete the task.

We have the example of Mozart to illustrate the principle. He said in one of his letters that his inspiration came suddenly as a fully completed piece of work. It appeared in his mind as a whole. The tedious task was then to write it out in linear form, note for note, and it was this linear expression that was, in his words, "Motzartish," like his nose. If the listener has the insight to hear the work "as a whole," the original inspiration emerges and we are lifted out of the ordinary into the sublime.

We are able to see now that in fact a method emerges in what appears to be disjointed. This section of Instinct and Inspiration, defined earlier, is now illustrated for the student. And it is power that takes center stage now. "Power is the authentic mark of spirit." The illustration comes, as it often does with Emerson, from the Neoplatonists, in this case Proclus. "The parts in us are more the property of wholes, and of things above us, than they are our property." The use of terms like parts, wholes, and products may appear mundane, but Emerson is trying to reach us, to help us see that what we ignorantly conceive of as our own powers belong to a higher source. We are in it; it is not in us—and yet it is, in a sense, in that the power comes through us as long as our instruments are well-assembled and in good tune.

If we ask how this power is taught or developed in our children, we are told to abstain, to withhold our intrusions into their lives. Nature is in charge and the less we do to stand in Her way the better. The games of children are for exploring Nature in all its forms, and we must step back and encourage, support, and protect. If our very own thoughts don't belong to us and arise as they will, how can we direct the child with our will?

III. OUR PATHETIC INTELLECT

Emerson writes, "I know not why, but our thoughts have a life of their own, independent of our will." He knows that thoughts arise unbidden, with a life of their own, but he claims he doesn't know why. I suspect he knew exactly why, but then, less was known in 1870 about the unconscious. He then continues. "Intellect is universal, not individual," then calls this fact 'pathetic.' Of the various meanings of pathetic, such as sad and sorrowful, pathetic also can mean contemptibly inadequate. This latter assessment of our lack of individual intellect, is ironic on Emerson's part.

As an Idealist, he exults in the universality of Intellect, that connection to the universal that makes us one with the cosmos and universal Mind. But still, he appears to complain that our lack of individuality is mildly depressing, so subject are we to unbidden thoughts that intrude upon what we like to think is controlled personal thought. But as any sane person will admit, thoughts do arise independent of our desire to keep them suppressed. It is a lesson learned by anyone who has practiced meditation.

In the art of meditation, the object is stillness of mind, a grateful silence within which the meditator becomes one with the greater stillness. Efforts to suppress the busy mind vary from the use of a mantra, to a focus on the breathing, or attention focused on the body, external sounds, or by simply watching thoughts as they come and go until, hopefully, quiet reigns.

IV. TRUSTING THE UNKNOWN THOUGHT

One of Emerson's finest connections between Nature and the powers of Intellect appears here in his observation that ninety percent of a tree's nourishment comes from the air, the invisible air we breathe and take in for our own lives. The tree takes carbon from the carbon dioxide molecule, strips out the carbon to use for growth, and then emits oxygen into the atmosphere, the same oxygen which we use and then emit carbon dioxide in return.

It turns out, then, that what appears to be the tree's total dependence on soil, sun, and water is an illusion based on what we see superficially as opposed to what is truly happening. Leaves and branches are carbon-based and grow "out of thin air." The analogy is stated as "Not the less are the arts and institutions of men created out of thought." And all that we see in human affairs arise from an idea, the thin air of thought. It is oxygen that builds bridges.

What we take from this imagery is something of the mystery that builds us and feeds us as human beings. Emerson analogizes to reach the principle that "the world is intellectual," and so are we. We receive our knowledge through our genius, the Intellect as pervasive force. The challenge confronts us when society or other persons seek to impose their values and certainties upon our genius, to thwart our instincts. Here is how Emerson phrased the principle in "Spiritual Laws,"

> There is guidance for each of us, and by lowly listening we shall hear the right word. Why need you choose so painfully your place, and occupation, and associates, and modes of action, and of entertainment? Certainly there is a possible right for you that precludes the need of balance and wilful election. For you there is a reality, a fit place and congenial duties. Place yourself in the middle of the stream of power and wisdom

which animates all whom it floats, and you are without effort
impelled to truth, to right, and a perfect contentment.

This more poetic articulation sermonizes rather than philosophizes—less argument and more encouragement, we might say—and this earlier essay from thirty years before serves to illustrate the later shift to more philosophical syntax.

V. SERVING OUR GENIUS

Carrying on this theme Emerson reminds us that when we delight in the work we do, we have found our genius no matter what the work, what its measure in society. This principle goes all the way back to Plato, whose search for justice in the "Republic" concludes with the revelation that true justice exists when every person finds and does his and her own work and never intrudes upon the proper work of another.

Emerson admits that people do not always find their aim or the task that they are best to perform, but he urges us to search until the right work finds us. When it does not then failure results and as he says, life becomes a kind of hibernation. What is encouraging, however, is the notion or principle that either we will find our true work or it will find us. Keeping that principle in mind and being honest in our assessment of what we are doing in the meantime, is crucial.

As a personal admission (rare for Emerson) he recounts his own struggle to follow his own star and still stay connected to the people closest to him. His chosen image is this account in the theater, where each of us has opportunity on the stage to say our piece.

Men generally attempt, early in life, to make their brothers,
afterwards their wives, acquainted with what is going forward

in their private theatre; but they soon desist from the attempt,
in finding that they also have some farce, or, perhaps, some
ear-and heart-rending tragedy forward on their secret boards,
on which they are intent; and all parties acquiesce, at last,
each in a private box, with the whole play performed before
himself solus.

In this instance he refers to his two brothers, Edward and
Charles who both died too young, and then to his wife Lidian,
with whom he lived for nearly fifty years. That we are alone in
our journey, in our interior journey, is evident. We can never
quite get our story out, true even for those who are the most
loquacious and extravagant in their explanations, which sound
more like the lines from a play than any true account of our
being.

Emerson ends this theme on Instinct and Inspiration with a
simple plea for perseverance, the effort to keep at it, never to
cease from exploration as Eliot phrased it; but we will let Emerson finish it: "There is but one only liberator in this life from the
demons that invade us, and that is, Endeavor,—earnest, entire,
perennial endeavor." And this quality is a truly human one.

VI. THE INTEGRITY OF THE INTELLECT

In this context Emerson chooses not to attack traditional religion directly. What he offers first is the principle that Intellect
possesses a severe truth, with "virtues more costly than any
Bible has consecrated." He then moves beyond the Bible to
challenge the culture's various images and traditions surround-
ing the persona of God. He says "I will think the truth against
what is called God."

And here are his thoughts, and incidentally, as they are our
thoughts as well.

If immortality, in the sense in which you seek it, is best, you shall be immortal. If it is up to the dignity of that order of things you know, it is secure. The sky, the sea, the plants, the rocks, astronomy, chemistry, keep their word. Morals and the genius of humanity will also. In short, the whole moral of modern science is the transference of that trust which is felt in Nature's admired arrangements, to the sphere of freedom and of rational life.

His first thought in this passage comes from his essay entitled "Immortality," and the key proviso "if it is for the best" moves our thoughts from beliefs and wishes to a serious consideration of the realities of whatever we conceive to be the actual details of an eternal life. Nature, he says, keeps its word, and we had better look with a clear eye at what that word is. I find the final sentence of that paragraph to be one of Emerson's finest philosophical definitions of Idealism.

Consider it. Begin at the end. What is rational life, what is freedom, and what is the sphere of the two? Our freedom comes with self-trust. Emerson said that he had spirits in prison whom no one visited if he did not. These were his people and their task was to find the freedom of independent thought: personal thought from the Instinct and Inspiration of the Intellect. Rational thought meant without fantasy, or from a derelict imagination. From the two molded into a perfect sphere came wisdom and sanity.

Then, the beginning. Morality and science. It is not reductionist science that serves but that science which grasps the moral implications of its role in advancing the truth as we come to know it. It is a science respectful of Nature and its laws, not a science that destroys or manipulates for private gain or tramples on life for that same private gain.

Then, the core of the sentence: "the transference of that trust which is felt in Nature's admired arrangements." The arrangements that we admire most are self-supporting ecologies, symbiosis, refulgence, endurance, and patience. Therefore, Idealism here is the trust we admire in Nature transferred to the human mind to create and sustain a free and rational life. And the process of transference takes place because the human mind has access to Nature's mind, and that is the core knowledge of Idealism.

3.

Memory

Memory, Emerson tells us, "is the thread upon which the beads of man are strung, making the personal identity which is necessary to moral action." Without the proper functioning of memory, with breaking of that thread through injury or decay, the rest of our faculties fall to the ground like precious beads and are lost. Emerson's image makes the point that faculties like imagination, perception, analysis, reason, and creativity, may remain unharmed, but when memory fades away, we cannot place any of the other functions in order with others from the past, nor can we judge the worth or wisdom of a thought in the context that memory supplies and preserves for us.

Instead of merely a savings bank or storehouse, memory is an instructor "with a prophetic sense of values." As we age, faces, names, and places disappear, perhaps to rise again in odd moments, but what never fades away are principles and moral values. We always remember what love is, even when we forget the lover.

The importance of the memory is engraved in the mythology of the Greeks. It is Memory (Mnemosyne) who sleeps with

Zeus for nine days and gives birth to nine daughters, who are the Muses. They represent Epic song, lyric song, sacred song, poetry, dance, tragedy, comedy, astronomy, and history. The latter two seem strange to us now, but astronomy and its concomitant astrology were considered as arts, as was the writing of history, being more than a recording of names, places, dates, and events. Emerson said that real history is the record of the One Mind; and of course, history was also the official record of memory, the mother of the muses.

Human beings are plagued with the tension between originality and memory. We think we have an original thought, something new under the sun, only to discover that we are plagiarizers, that our thought is as old as thought itself. But as long as the string of words used to form this "new" thought is not the same as the original, we are excused and are merely humbled. Such is the importance of memory. Society could never meliorate but through the grace and example of memory.

But then memory is also not our friend. It behaves badly, as Emerson says, like an old aunt who comes into the house and recites an old refrain and then slips out the back door. Historically, memory was revered and regarded as sacred. "Plato deplores writing as a barbarous invention which would weaken the memory by disuse."

In our own time, our digital world of instantly retrievable information, memory suffers even more. Rote learning in school has disappeared from the lesson plans. We now pretend to teach students how to think, but few teachers know what that even means. How can we say with Emerson that memory is the thread upon which the beads of mind are strung? His answer to that question comes as a principle in architecture: "An arch never sleeps." It bears its weight as long as the building lasts.

The memory never sleeps either. It may let facts slip away, but it seeks to preserve continuity in the life. There is something in Emerson's more relaxed, almost homey, tone through this section, that suggests a sense of reminiscence, a recognition of his own fading memory, which was already evident and would abandon him several years later as an example of Alzheimer's. His daughter Ellen came into his study one day and found her father reading an old essay of his as if for the first time. He commented that it seemed quite good. We gently say that the mooring was loosed by the storm of life and the boat quietly drifted out to sea.

The positive nature of the operations of memory is that it "has a fine art of sifting out the pain and keeping all the joy." Is this wishful thinking or the way the human system maintains a survival strategy? Emerson's old friend Sampson Reed said, "The true way to store the memory is to develop the affections," to which Emerson comments, "Remember me means, Do not cease to love me."

At the close of this approximation of the Harvard Lectures, these mere fragments of those seven lectures he was able to offer, we have a sense of his method, his vision of Idealism. He says in his conclusion, "When we live by principles instead of traditions, by obedience to the law of the mind instead of by passion, the Great Mind will enter into us, not as now in frag-ments and detached thoughts, but the light of to-day will shine backward and forward."

He resisted to the end the linear, calculated formalism of the schoolmen's lecture format. It has been said that Emerson invented the public lecture, the sheets of notes, the reflective pause, the straying from the stated topic, the sharing in the moment of a new thought, and, of course, the recall from memory of a anecdote to illustrate a principle. It was the best he could do to let the Great Mind lead him, to get himself out of the way, to learn as the audience did, what that mind wanted to impart.

This method is reflected as well in all his essays and gives to generations of readers a glimpse of the Idealism that he cherished all his life.

A Brief History of Emerson's Ideas on Mind

In this "brief history" I wish to describe the key references to Universal Mind in Emerson's life and work. As I shall illustrate, from the time he began using a journal at age sixteen in his junior year at Harvard, Emerson associated the word Mind (capitalized) with God in a religious context, gradually shifted his thinking to a more Neoplatonic characterization, and eventually made the attempt to bring Mind into some sense of scientific context. What appears below is not comprehensive. Rather the examples show a progression of thought and expression, which I hope will be useful to those who may be exploring similar reasoning.

As early as age seventeen, Emerson possessed an idea of a universal mind. It may have come from a book written in 1813 entitled *Philosophy of the Mind* by Dugald Stewart. Here is a first reference to an uppercase use of Mind from his journals:

Of all the sciences the science of the Mind is necessarily the most worthy and elevating. But it cannot precede the others.

Natural Philosophy and Mathematics must be sought in order
to gain first, the comforts of civilized life, and then the data
whence our moral reasonings proceed.

Here is Emerson at age nineteen, still firmly connected to a
religious context in reference to a greater Mind:

The child who refuses to pollute its little lips with a lie, and
the archangel who refuses with indignation to rebel in the
armies of heaven against the Most High, act alike in obedi-
ence to a law which pervades all intelligent beings. This law
is the Moral Sense; a rule coextensive and coeval with Mind.
It derives its existence from the eternal character of the Deity
. . . Whence comes this strong universal feeling that approves
or abhors actions? Manifestly not from matter, which is alto-
gether unmoved by it, and the connection of which with it is
a thing absurd—but from a Mind, of which it is the essence.
That Mind is God.

Then he sees something diminished in the greater Mind
compared to the human mind:

Mind, from being the free born citizen of the Universe and
the inheritor of glory, has become the caterer and the pander
of sense.

This decline will appear in *Nature* in the idea of man as a god
in ruins. Meanwhile, Emerson is reading and gathering what he
called "lustres" from a variety of sources, one of which during
this period was Sampson Reed's *Growth of the Mind*. He was
also reading Plutarch.

At age twenty-seven, in 1830, Emerson makes a significant
entry in his journal, one that begins to change his entire concept
of mind. The source is Plutarch on Anaxagoras, who was the

first philosopher to practice his art in Athens. Here is the entry, under Anaxagoras:

> Plutarch remarks "that the Contemporaries of Anaxagoras gave him the surname of Nous (mind) because he first had disengaged it from all mixture, presented it in all its simplicity, and its purity, and placed it at the summits of all being." I think this a very remarkable passage of the history of philosophy, as it casts light upon the disengagement also of the idea of God; for the greatest problem of the history of opinions is whether this idea is reasoned out or revealed. Anaxagoras taught at Athens, but is reckoned in the Ionian School because, like them, he cultivated the Physical Sciences. But the great merit of Anaxagoras is thus told. Whilst the system of emanations, the systems of Pantheism, the opinions of the first Ionians themselves, had associated the elementary matter of all things to the first cause of all production, and thus conceive the Divinity as the universal soul, the soul of the world, the world itself as an animated whole identical in some sort with its author, Anaxagoras first detached, separated with precision and neatness these two notions until then confounded. The Universe is in his eyes an effect wholly distinct from its Cause.
>
> This Cause has nothing common with the rest of beings. It hath its peculiar nature, one, eternal, acts on the world as workman on materials. So the idea of the first Cause, which until then was essentially defined by the attribute of Power, was determined by Anaxagoras to receive chiefly the attribute of intelligence.

From this observation comes Emerson's use of the word Intellect to represent the Greek concept of Nous, or universal mind.

BIOGRAPHICAL NOTE

The period from 1830 through 1836 for Emerson was turbulent and life-changing. He completed his studies at Divinity College, qualifying him to receive an appointment as Junior Minister of Second Church, Boston. He became engaged to Ellen Tucker, aged seventeen from Concord, New Hampshire, and they were married in 1829. At age nineteen Ellen died of tuberculosis on February 9, 1831, leaving Emerson bereft. He resigned from Second Church, sold his belongings, and sailed for Europe on Christmas Day, 1831. He traveled through Italy, Switzerland, France, and England. With letters of introduction he met with Coleridge and Wordsworth, but was disappointed in both elderly men. His meeting with Carlyle, however, proved inspiring and important for a lifetime. He returned to America and in 1833 settled in Concord, Massachusetts, where he determined to begin a career lecturing and writing. In 1835, he married Lydia Jackson of Plymouth and moved into the house that remained their home until his death in 1882. It remains The Emerson House Museum to this day.

In 1836, Emerson published *Nature*. This quote is from the last chapter, "Prospects."

> *'The foundations of man are not in matter, but in spirit. But the element of spirit is eternity. To it, therefore, the longest series of events, the oldest chronologies are young and recent. In the cycle of the universal man, from whom the known individuals proceed, centuries are points, and all history is but the epoch of one degradation.*
>
> *'We distrust and deny inwardly our sympathy with nature. We own and disown our relation to it, by turns. We are, like Nebuchadnezzar, dethroned, bereft of reason, and eating grass like an ox. But who can set limits to the remedial force of spirit?*

'*A man is a god in ruins. When men are innocent, life shall be longer, and shall pass into the immortal, as gently as we awake from dreams. Now, the world would be insane and rabid, if these disorganizations should last for hundreds of years. It is kept in check by death and infancy. Infancy is the perpetual Messiah, which comes into the arms of fallen men, and pleads with them to return to paradise.*

'*Man is the dwarf of himself. Once he was permeated and dissolved by spirit. He filled nature with his overflowing currents. Out from him sprang the sun and moon; from man, the sun; from woman, the moon. The laws of his mind, the periods of his actions externized themselves into day and night, into the year and the seasons. But, having made for himself this huge shell, his waters retired; he no longer fills the veins and veinlets; he is shrunk to a drop. He sees, that the structure still fits him, but fits him colossally. Say, rather, once it fitted him, now it corresponds to him from far and on high. He adores timidly his own work. Now is man the follower of the sun, and woman the follower of the moon. Yet sometimes he starts in his slumber, and wonders at himself and his house, and muses strangely at the resemblance betwixt him and it. He perceives that if his law is still paramount, if still he have elemental power, if his word is sterling yet in nature, it is not conscious power, it is not inferior but superior to his will. It is Instinct.*' Thus my Orphic poet sang.

After this, Emerson sets out to lecture and write. His next publication is *Essays, First Series*, published in 1841. The series begins with "History" and this is its first sentence:

There is one mind common to all individual men.

Here appears mind in lower case, resulting in some ambiguity as to its meaning. Some have assumed he meant something like Jung's collective unconscious; it seems clear that he means a universal Mind, but is being somewhat coy in setting out on that path, at least divorced from a religious context.

Next in this volume is "Self-Reliance," which is the central essay of his career and the essay that is most deeply misread at a number of levels. As to Mind, however, we see in this next key sentence a suggestion that Mind will be the basis of Idealism, or as we sometimes call it New England Transcendentalism.

Nothing is, at last, sacred but the integrity of your own mind.

This sentence has caused great confusion among both readers and scholars. Emerson's intent, however, is clear. The word "integrity" means whole, unified, spherical. When the human mind possesses that integrity, then the world and the universe will be sacred. But it is Mind that is the sacred source of that integrity.

Next, in the third essay in this series, "Compensation," he uses the expression "Supreme Mind," but he couches it in Greek myth:

The human soul is true to these facts in the painting of fable, of history, of law, of proverbs, of conversation. It finds a tongue in literature unawares. Thus the Greeks called Jupiter, Supreme Mind;

It's Zeus, of course, not the Roman Jupiter, and we see references in literature to Zeus as Great Consciousness rather than Mind. Athena—Wisdom—was born fully grown from the forehead of her father Zeus. In this imagery we understand Wisdom to be an attribute of the gods and not merely a human virtue.

In "The Over-Soul" we have an intensely poetic assertion of the nature of a universal mind—disguised as Critic, but then described as Mind. Emerson's decision to use the term "Over-

Soul" rather than Supreme Mind, Great Mind, etc., maintains a quasi-religious connection to traditional belief but also establishes new ground with the word "Over."

> *The Supreme Critic on the errors of the past and the present, and the only prophet of that which must be, is that great nature in which we rest, as the earth lies in the soft arms of the atmosphere; that Unity, that Over-soul, within which every man's particular being is contained and made one with all other; that common heart, of which all sincere conversation is the worship, to which all right action is submission; that overpowering reality which confutes our tricks and talents, and constrains every one to pass for what he is, and to speak from his character, and not from his tongue, and which evermore tends to pass into our thought and hand, and become wisdom, and virtue, and power, and beauty. We live in succession, in division, in parts, in particles. Meantime within man is the soul of the whole; the wise silence; the universal beauty, to which every part and particle is equally related; the eternal ONE. . . .*
>
> *The lover has no talent, no skill, which passes for quite nothing with his enamoured maiden, however little she may possess of related faculty; and the heart which abandons itself to the Supreme Mind finds itself related to all its works, and will travel a royal road to particular knowledges and powers. In ascending to this primary and aboriginal sentiment, we have come from our remote station on the circumference instantaneously to the centre of the world, where, as in the closet of God, we see causes, and anticipate the universe, which is but a slow effect.*

Later, in a *Dial* article entitled "Thoughts on Modern Literature," Emerson used the expression the One Mind. This usage makes a small change from the "one mind" of "History."

Of the perception now fast becoming a conscious fact,—that there is One Mind, and that all the powers and privileges which lie in any, lie in all; that I, as a man, may claim and appropriate whatever of true or fair or good or strong has anywhere been exhibited; that Moses and Confucius, Montage and Leibnitz, are not so much individuals as they are parts of man and parts of me, and my intelligence proves them my own,—literature is far the best expression.

This difference between the capitalized Mind and the lowercase mind is significant. We see in the Emerson Concordance of the Complete Works that Emerson used the lowercase 'mind' over 1,100 times but capitalized it only four times used by itself.

In 1860, in the essay "Beauty" Emerson uses the upper case when he writes,

Wherever we begin, thither our steps tend: an ascent from the joy of a horse in his trappings, up to the perception of Newton, that the globe on which we ride is only a larger apple falling from a larger tree; up to the perception of Plato, that globe and universe are rude and early expressions of an all-dissolving Unity,—the first stair on the scale to the temple of the Mind.

In 1862, Emerson uses the term Divine Mind, although buried in an essay entitled "Character." He does not stay with the term, but goes straight on to the individual among other individuals:

The Divine Mind imparts itself to the single person: his whole duty is to this rule and teaching. The aid which others give us is like that of the mother to the child,—temporary, gestative, a short period of lactation, a nurse's or a governess's care; but on his arrival at a certain maturity, it ceases, and would be hurtful and ridiculous if prolonged.

Also in the 1862 volume of essays, in "Education" he uses the term Grand Mind.

The great object of Education should be commensurate with the object of life. It should be a moral one; to teach self-trust: to inspire the youthful man with an interest in himself ; with a curiosity touching his own nature; to acquaint him with the resources of his mind, and to teach him that there is all his strength, and to inflame him with a piety towards the Grand Mind in which he lives.

In 1867, Emerson delivered an address to the Organization of Free Religious Association, in which he declared the relationship of the universal Mind to the Trinity and to the individual mind.

The Holy Ghost and the Son of Mary were worshipped, and in the thirteenth century, the First Person began to appear at the side of his Son, in pictures and in sculpture, for worship, but only through favor of his Son. These mortifying puerilities abound in religious history. But as soon as every man is apprised of the Divine Presence within his own mind, —is apprised that the perfect law of duty corresponds with the laws of chemistry, of vegetation, of astronomy, as face to face in a glass; that the basis of duty, the order of society, the power of character, the wealth of culture, the perfection of taste, all draw their essence from this moral sentiment, then we have a religion that exalts, that commands all the social and all the private action.

Here is a reference to Emerson's gradual connection of universal mind to science and to empirical evidence which he saw emerging. It is at about this time in his life that Emerson seeks overtly to make the connection between what was once exclusively a religious symbol and is now a scientific theory to be empirically proven at some point.

The final reference to the universal mind occurs in the Memory section of "Natural History of Intellect." In fact it is Emerson's last word from his lectures at Harvard in 1871.

When we live by principles instead of traditions, by obedience to the law of the mind instead of by passion, the Great Mind will enter into us, not as now in fragments and detached thoughts, but the light of today will shine backward and forward.

As the preceding essay has shown, Emerson used the symbol "Intellect" to stand for the higher faculty of the human mind corresponding to or linked to the Greater Mind. This device gave him a mode of writing and expression freeing him from some of the connotations of Mind, Greater Mind, and so on used earlier. Therefore, the title "Natural History of Intellect" could be presented as fresh territory in the landscape of Idealism.

The Platonic Philosopher's Creed

1 | I BELIEVE that there is one first cause of all things, whose nature is so immensely transcendent, that it is even superessential; and that in consequence of this it cannot properly either be named or spoken of, or conceived by opinion, or be known, or perceived by any being.

2 | I believe, however, that if it be lawful to give a name to that which is truly ineffable, the appellations of The One and The Good are of all others the most adapted to it; the former of these names indicating that it is the principle of all things, and the latter that it is the ultimate object of desire to all things.

3 | I believe that this immense principle produced such things as are first and proximate to itself, most similar to itself;

This statement of beliefs, or creed, was written by Thomas Taylor, Platonist and translator of Plato's works and those of the Neoplatonists. Emerson was devoted to Taylor's work and used his translations for what he called the "lustres" of his study of Idealism.

just as the heat immediately proceeding from fire is most similar to the heat in the fire; and the light immediately emanating from the sun, to that which the sun essentially contains. Hence, this principle produces many principles proximately from itself.

4 | I likewise believe that since all things differ from each other, and are multiplied with their proper differences, each of these multitudes is suspended from its one proper principle. That, in consequence of this, all beautiful things, whether in souls or in bodies, are suspended from one fountain of beauty. That whatever possesses symmetry, and whatever is true, and all principles are in a certain respect connate with the first principle, so far as they are principles, with an appropriate subjection and analogy. That all other principles are comprehended in this first principle, not with interval and multitude, but as parts in the whole, and number in the monad. That it is not a certain principle like each of the rest; for of these, one is the principle of beauty, another of truth, and another of something else, but it is simply principle. Nor is it simply the principle of beings but it is the principle of principles: it being necessary that the characteristic property of principle after the same manner as other things, should not begin from multitude, but should be collected into one monad as a summit, and which is the principle of principles.

5 | I believe, therefore, that such things as are produced by the first good in consequence of being connascent with it, do not recede from essential goodness, since they are immovable and unchanged, and are eternally established in the same blessedness. All other natures, however, being

produced by the one good, and many goodnesses, since they fall off from essential goodness, and are not immovably established in the nature of divine goodness, possess on this account the good according to participation.

6 | I believe that as all things considered as subsisting causally in this immense principle, are transcendently more excellent than they are when considered as effects proceeding from him; this principle is very properly said to be all things, prior to all; priority denoting exempt transcendency. Just as number may be considered as subsisting occultly in the monad, and the circle in the centre; this occult being the same in each with causal subsistence.

7 | I believe that the most proper mode of venerating this great principle of principles is to extend in silence the ineffable parturitions of the soul to its ineffable co-sensation; and that if it be at all lawful to celebrate it, it is to be celebrated as a thrice unknown darkness, as the God of all Gods, and the unity of all unities, as more ineffable than all silence, and more occult than all essence, as holy among the holies, and concealed in its first progeny, the intelligible Gods.

8 | I believe that self-subsistent natures are the immediate offspring of this principle, if it be lawful thus to denominate things which ought rather to be called ineffable unfoldings into light from the ineffable.

9 | I believe that incorporeal forms or ideas resident in a divine intellect, are the paradigms or models of every thing which has a perpetual subsistence according to nature. That these ideas subsist primarily in the highest intellects, secondarily

in souls, and ultimately in sensible natures; and that they subsist in each, characterised by the essential properties of the beings in which they are contained. That they possess a paternal, producing, guardian, connecting, perfective and uniting power. That in divine beings they possess a power fabricative and gnostic; in nature a power fabricative but not gnostic: and in human souls in their present condition through a degradation of intellect, a power gnostic, but not fabricative.

10 | I believe that this world, depending on its divine artificer, who is himself an intelligible world, replete with the archetypal ideas of all things, is perpetually flowing, and perpetually advancing to being, and, compared with its paradigm, has no stability, or reality of being. That considered, however, as animated by a divine soul, and as being the receptacle of divinities from whom bodies are suspended, it is justly called by Plato, a blessed God.

11 | I believe that the great body of this world, which subsists in a perpetual dispersion of temporal extension, may be properly called a whole, with a total subsistence, or a whole of wholes, on account of the perpetuity of its duration, though this is nothing more than a flowing eternity. That the other wholes which it contains are the celestial spheres, the sphere of æther, the whole of air considered as one great orb, the whole earth, and the whole sea. That these spheres are parts with a total subsistence, and through this subsistence are perpetual.

12 | I believe that all the parts of the universe, are unable to participate of the providence of divinity in a similar

manner, but some of its parts enjoy this eternally, and others temporally; some in a primary and others in a secondary degree; for the universe being a perfect whole, must have a first, a middle, and a last part. But its first parts, as having the most excellent subsistence, must always exist according to nature; and its last parts must sometimes exist according to, and sometimes contrary to nature. Hence the celestial bodies, which are the first parts of the universe, perpetually subsist according to nature, both the whole spheres, and the multitude co-ordinate to these wholes; and the only alteration which they experience is a mutation of figure, and variation of light at different periods; but in the sublunary region, while the spheres of the elements remain on account of their subsistence, as wholes, always according to nature; the parts of the wholes have sometimes a natural, and sometimes an unnatural subsistence: for thus alone can the circle of generation unfold all the variety which it contains. The different periods therefore in which these mutations happen, are with great propriety called by Plato, periods of fertility and sterility: for in these periods a fertility or sterility of men, animals, and plants, takes place; so that in fertile periods mankind will be both more numerous, and upon the whole superior in mental and bodily endowments to the men of a barren period. And a similar reasoning must be extended to irrational animals and plants. The most dreadful consequence, likewise, attending a barren period with respect to mankind is this, that in such a period they have no scientific theology, and deny the existence of the immediate progeny of the ineffable cause of all things.

13 | I believe that as the divinities are eternally good and

profitable, but are never noxious, and ever subsist in the same uniform mode of being, we are conjoined with them through similitude when we are virtuous, but separated from them through dissimilitude when we are vicious. That while we live according to virtue we partake of the Gods, but cause them to be our enemies when we become evil: not that they are angry (for anger is a passion, and they are impassive), but because guilt prevents us from receiving the illuminations of the Gods, and subjects us to the power of dæmons of fateful justice. Hence, I believe, that if we obtain pardon of our guilt through prayers and sacrifices, we neither appease the Gods, nor cause any mutation to take place in them; but by methods of this kind, and by our conversion to a divine nature, we apply a remedy to our vices, and again become partakers of the goodness of the Gods. So that it is the same thing to assert, that divinity is turned from the evil, as to say that the sun is concealed from those who are deprived of sight.

14 | I believe that a divine nature is not indigent of any thing. But the honours which are paid to the Gods are performed for the sake of the advantage of those who pay them. Hence, since the providence of the Gods is extended every where, a certain habitude or fitness is all that is requisite for the reception of their beneficent communications. But all habitude is produced through imitation and similitude. On this account temples imitate the heavens, but altars the earth. Statues resemble life, and on this account they are similar to animals. Herbs and stones resemble matter; and animals which are sacrificed, the irrational life of our souls. From all these, however, nothing happens to the Gods beyond what they already possess; for what accession can

be made to a divine nature? But a conjunction of our souls
with the gods is by these means effected.

15 | I believe that as the world considered as one great
comprehending whole is a divine animal, so likewise every
whole which it contains is a world, possessing in the first
place a self-perfect unity proceeding from the ineffable,
by which it becomes a God; in the second place, a divine
intellect; in the third place, a divine soul; and in the last
place a deified body. That each of these wholes is the
producing cause of all the multitude which it contains, and
on this account is said to be a whole prior to parts; because
considered as possessing an eternal form which holds all
its parts together, and gives to the whole perpetuity of
subsistence, it is not indigent of such parts to the perfection
of its being. And it follows by a geometrical necessity, that
these wholes which rank thus high in the universe must
be animated.

16 | Hence I believe that after the immense principle of princi-
ples in which all things causally subsist absorbed in super-
essential light, and involved in unfathomable depths, a
beautiful series of principles proceeds, all largely partaking
of the ineffable, all stamped with the occult characters of
deity, all possessing an overflowing fullness of good. From
these dazzling summits, these ineffable blossoms, these
divine propagations—being, life, intellect, soul, nature
and body depend; monads suspended from unities, deified natures proceeding from deities. That each of these
monads is the leader of a series which extends to the last
of things, and which, while it proceeds from, at the same
time abides in, and returns to its leader. Thus all beings

proceed from, and are comprehended in the first being; all intellects emanate from one first intellect; all souls from one first soul; all natures blossom from one first nature; and all bodies proceed from the vital and luminous body of the world. That all these great monads are comprehended in the first one, from which both they and all their depending series are unfolded into light. And hence this first one is truly the unity of unities, the monad of monads, the principle of principles, the God of gods, one and all things, and yet one prior to all.

17 | I also believe, that of the Gods some are mundane, but others super-mundane; and that the mundane are those who fabricate the world. But of the supermundane, some produce essences, others intellect, and others soul; and on this account, they are distinguished into three orders. Of the mundane Gods also, some are the causes of the existence of the world; others animate it; others again harmonise it, thus composed of different natures; and lastly, others guard and preserve it when harmonically arranged. Since these orders are four, and each consists of things first, middle, and last, it is necessary that the governors of these should be twelve. Hence Zeus, Poseidon, and Hephaestus, fabricate the world; Demeter, Hera, and Artemis, animate it; Hermes, Aphrodite, and Apollo, harmonise it; and lastly, Hestia, Athena, and Ares, preside over it with a guardian power. But the truth of this, may be seen in statues, as in enigmas. For Apollo harmonises the lyre; Pallas Athena is invested with arms; and Aphrodite is naked; since harmony produces beauty, and beauty is not concealed in subjects of sensible inspection. I likewise believe that as

these Gods primarily possess the world, it is necessary to consider the other mundane Gods as subsisting in them; as Dionysius in Zeus, Aesculapius in Apollo, and the Graces in Aphrodite. We may also behold the spheres with which they are connected, viz. Hestia with the earth, Poseidon with water, Hera with air, and Hephaestus with fire. But Apollo and Artemis are assumed for the sun and moon; the sphere of Kronos is attributed to Demeter; Æther to Pallas; and heaven is common to them all.

18 | I also believe that man is a microcosm, comprehending in himself partially every thing which the world contains divinely and totally. That hence he is endued with an intellect subsisting in energy, and a rational soul proceeding from the same causes as those from which the intellect and soul of the universe proceed. And that he has likewise an ethereal vehicle analogous to the heavens, and a terrestrial body composed from the four elements, and with which also it is co-ordinate.

19 | I believe that the rational part of man, in which his essence consists, is of a selfmotive nature, and that it subsists between intellect, which is immovable both in essence and energy, and nature, which both moves and is moved.

20 | I believe that the human as well as every mundane soul, uses periods and restitutions of its proper life. For in consequence of being measured by time, it energizes transitively, and possesses a proper motion. But every thing which is moved perpetually, and participates of time, revolves periodically, and proceeds from the same to the same.

21 | I also believe that as the human soul ranks among the number of those souls that sometimes follow the mundane divinities, in consequence of subsisting immediately after angels, dæmons and heroes the perpetual attendants of the Gods, it possesses a power of descending infinitely into the sublunary region, and of ascending from thence to real being. That in consequence of this, the soul, while an inhabitant of earth, is in a fallen condition, an apostate from deity, an exile from the orb of light. That she can only be restored, while on earth, to the divine likeness, and be able after death to re-ascend to the intelligible world, by the exercise of the cathartic, and theoretic virtues; the former purifying her from the defilements of a mortal nature, and the latter elevating her to the vision of true being. And that such a soul returns after death to her kindred star from which she fell, and enjoys a blessed life.

22 | I believe that the human soul essentially contains all knowledge, and that whatever knowledge she acquires in the present life, is nothing more than a recovery of what she once possessed; and which discipline evocates from its dormant retreats.

23 | I also believe that the soul is punished in a future for the crimes she has committed in the present life; but that this punishment is proportioned to the crimes, and is not perpetual; divinity punishing, not from anger or revenge, but in order to purify the guilty soul, and restore her to the proper perfection of her nature.

24 | I also believe that the human soul on its departure from the present life, will, if not properly purified, pass into

other terrene bodies; and that if it passes into a human body, it becomes the soul of that body; but if into the body of a brute, it does not become the soul of the brute, but is externally connected with the brutal soul in the same manner as presiding dæmons are connected, in their beneficent operations, with mankind; for the rational part never becomes the soul of the irrational nature.

25 | Lastly, I believe that souls that live according to virtue, shall in other respects be happy; and when separated from the irrational nature, and purified from all body, shall be conjoined with the Gods, and govern the whole world, together with the deities by whom it was produced.

Endnotes

1. James Elliot Cabot, *A Memoir of Ralph Waldo Emerson,* VOL II (London & New York: Macmillian & Co., 1887, p. 251).

2. Readers interested in having the text of "Natural History of Intellect" may find it online at www.RWE.org. The file may be copy/pasted into any word processor.

3. In an article published May 19, 2012 by BigQuestionsOnline, Stephen Barr examines the relationship of quantum mechanics and mind. He explains why the existence of a universal mind is a requirement for the measurable evidence of quantum behavior. It is typical of many good articles and books exploring the presence of consciousness as a universal substance or entity. Accessed May 19, 2012 at https://www.bigquestionsonline.com/content/does-quantum-physics-make-it-easier-believe-god

4. Robert D. Richardson, Jr., *Emerson: The Mind on Fire* (Berkeley and Los Angeles: University of California Press, 1996, p. 51).

5. Barbara L. Packer, *Emerson's Fall* (London & New York: Continuum International Publishing Group, 1982)

6. Kathleen Raine and George Mills Harper, *Thomas Taylor the Platonist* (New York: Bollingen Foundation, 1969).

7. Van Wyck Brooks, *The Life of Emerson* (New York: The Literary Guild, 1932, p. 298).

8. Emerson's emphasis on seeing was also a recommendation by Ludwig Wittgenstein, who believed strongly that in philosophy, seeing was more than thinking. "Don't think, look!" he said in *Philosophical Investigations.* [See article by Ray Monk in the

New Statesman, Aug. 15, 2012 <http://www.newstatesman.com/culture/art-and-design/2012/08/ludwig-wittgenstein%E2%80%99s-passion-looking-not-thinking> accessed May 18, 2012]

9. We learn from Emerson's biographers that by 1871 Emerson's powers had diminished and his daughter Ellen had to help him organize his papers and stand with him at the lectern. In the dim light she had to hold a lantern or candle nearby so that he could see the text. It could not have been an easy time or an effective teaching moment for him.

10. James S. Grotstein, *Who is the Dreamer, Who Dreams the Dream* (London and New York: Routledge, 2000.

11. Alexander Pope, *An Essay on Criticism,* Part II

About the Author

Richard G. Geldard is a full-time writer and lecturer living in New York City and the Hudson Valley. His primary contribution to Emerson studies is in making difficult texts accessible to serious readers. Before turning to writing he was an educator, teaching English and philosophy at the secondary, undergraduate, and graduate levels. His most recent appointment is with the philosophy faculty of the University of Philosophical Research in their online Masters degree program. Prior to that he was on the graduate faculty of the Pacifica Graduate Institute in California, and Yeshiva College in New York. He is a graduate of Bowdoin College, The Bread Loaf School of English at Middlebury College and Stanford University, where he earned his doctorate in Dramatic Literature and Classics in 1972. He has also studied at St. John's College, Oxford. Dr. Geldard is the author of ten books, including studies of Ralph Waldo Emerson and Greek philosophy and culture.